The Development Dimension

This book critically analyses the World Trade Organization's (WTO's) approach to "special and differential treatment" (SDT) to argue that it is founded on seeking exemptions from WTO obligations, instead of creating an enabling environment for developing countries to integrate fully into the multilateral trading system. Through six key sections:

- United States proposal on special and differential treatment
- Responses to the United States proposal
- The evolution of differential treatment
- Failure of the current approach to differential treatment
- Complications created by China's emergence in the global economy
- An alternative approach to differential treatment

This book explores how, by adopting a new evidence-based, case-by-case approach to SDT, the development of the poorest countries can best be advanced, while at the same time ensuring that advanced developing countries carry their weight in the organisation.

It will be of interest to scholars and students of international trade law and political science, as well as trade practitioners such as lawyers, diplomats, and analysts.

James Bacchus is a Distinguished University Professor of Global Affairs and Director of the Center for Global Economic and Environmental Opportunity at the University of Central Florida in Orlando, Florida, USA, and an Adjunct Scholar at the Cato Institute in Washington DC, USA. Inu Manak is a Research Fellow at the Cato Institute in Washington DC, USA.

Insights on International Economic Law
Series Editor: David Collins, Professor of International Economic Law at City, University of London.

International Economic Law is among the fastest growing and vibrant fields of international law, responding to the escalating tensions in global trade and investment which take on not only economic and legal but also social and geopolitical dimensions. In many respects the issues of International Economic Law are among the most important of our times, as captured for example in the ongoing fascination with the trade aspects of Brexit, the US–China trade war, security-related fears of foreign investment in critical infrastructure projects and the controversial elements of China's economic expansion into the developing world. The Routledge Insights on International Economic Law series is an important conduit for the dissemination of crucial, socially valuable research, encompassing peer reviewed short-form style books which examine emerging hot topics in international economic law which have reached a pivotal stage of importance.

The Development Dimension
Special and Differential
Treatment in Trade

James Bacchus and Inu Manak

LONDON AND NEW YORK

First published 2021
by Routledge
2 Park Square, Milton Park, Abingdon, Oxon OX14 4RN

and by Routledge
52 Vanderbilt Avenue, New York, NY 10017

Routledge is an imprint of the Taylor & Francis Group, an informa business

© 2021 James Bacchus and Inu Manak

The right of James Bacchus and Inu Manak to be identified as authors of this work has been asserted by them in accordance with sections 77 and 78 of the Copyright, Designs and Patents Act 1988.

All rights reserved. No part of this book may be reprinted or reproduced or utilised in any form or by any electronic, mechanical, or other means, now known or hereafter invented, including photocopying and recording, or in any information storage or retrieval system, without permission in writing from the publishers.

Trademark notice: Product or corporate names may be trademarks or registered trademarks, and are used only for identification and explanation without intent to infringe.

British Library Cataloguing-in-Publication Data
A catalogue record for this book is available from the British Library

Library of Congress Cataloging-in-Publication Data
Names: Bacchus, Jim, 1949- author. | Manak, Inu, author.
Title: The development dimension: special and differential treatment in trade/James Bacchus and Inu Manak.
Description: Milton Park, Abingdon, Oxon: New York, NY: Routledge, 2021. | Series: Insights on international economic law | Includes bibliographical references and index.
Identifiers: LCCN 2020050930 (print) | LCCN 2020050931 (ebook) | ISBN 9780367710903 (hardback) | ISBN 9781003165521 (ebook)
Subjects: LCSH: World Trade Organization. | Trade regulation–Developing countries. | Developing countries–Commerce.
Classification: LCC K4610 .B333 2021 (print) | LCC K4610 (ebook) | DDC 382/.92091724–dc23
LC record available at https://lccn.loc.gov/2020050930
LC ebook record available at https://lccn.loc.gov/2020050931

ISBN: 978-0-367-71090-3 (hbk)
ISBN: 978-0-367-76108-0 (pbk)
ISBN: 978-1-003-16552-1 (ebk)

Typeset in Times New Roman
by KnowledgeWorks Global Ltd.

Contents

About the authors vi

1 Introduction 1

2 United States proposal on special and differential treatment 6

3 Responses to the United States proposal 12

4 The evolution of differential treatment 23

5 Failure of the current approach to differential treatment 34

6 Complications created by China's emergence in the global economy 45

7 An alternative approach to differential treatment 55

8 Conclusion 76

Index 77

About the authors

James Bacchus, Distinguished University Professor of Global Affairs and Director of the Center for Global Economic and Environmental Opportunity at the University of Central Florida, Florida, was a founding judge and was twice the Chairman—the chief judge—of the highest court of world trade, the Appellate Body of the WTO in Geneva, Switzerland. He is a former Member of the Congress of the United States, from Florida, and a former international trade negotiator for the United States. He is an Adjunct Scholar of the Cato Institute in Washington and a Global Fellow of the Centre for International Governance Innovation in Canada. He served on the High-Level Advisory Panel to the Conference of Parties of the United Nations Framework Convention on Climate Change, chaired the global Commission on Trade and Investment Policy of the International Chamber of Commerce, chaired the global sustainability council of the World Economic Forum, and is a member of the Advisory Board for the United States chapter of the United Nations Sustainable Development Solutions Network. He is the Pao Yue-Kong Chair Professor at Zhejiang University in Hangzhou, China. For more than 14 years, he chaired the global practice of the largest law firm in the United States and one of the largest in the world. He is a frequent writer in leading publications and a frequent speaker on prominent platforms worldwide.

Inu Manak, Research Fellow at the Cato Institute, Washington, DC, USA, is an expert in international political economy, with a specialisation in international trade policy and law. Dr. Manak's research focuses on the WTO, non-judicial treaty mechanisms, technical barriers to trade, regional trade agreements, and development. Dr. Manak is a participating scholar in the Robert A. Pastor North American Research Initiative, a joint program between American

University's Center for Latin American and Latino Studies and the School of International Service. She is also a Book Review Editor for *World Trade Review*. Previously, she was a Junior Visiting Fellow at the Centre for Trade and Economic Integration at the Graduate Institute and Fellow at TradeLab, a Geneva- based NGO, which assists developing countries, SMEs and NGOs build legal capacity in trade and investment law. She earned a PhD in government at Georgetown University.

1 Introduction

On July 26, 2019, President Donald Trump levelled yet another in the lengthening series of his taunts by tweet at the World Trade Organization (WTO). This time, he complained that developing countries are given an unfair advantage in trade with the United States and other developed countries because of the special and differential treatment (SDT) they receive as WTO Members, stating "The WTO is BROKEN when the world's RICHEST countries claim to be developing countries to avoid WTO rules and get special treatment. No more!!! Today I directed the U.S. Trade Representative to take action so that countries stop CHEATING the system at the expense of the USA!"[1]

As we shall explain, President Trump was right that SDT in the WTO must be changed, but he was wrong about the reason why. Developing countries are not "cheating" by availing themselves of their rights to SDT, which is expressly permitted by WTO rules. Moreover, developed countries have previously agreed to this different trade treatment for developing countries. This said, the provision of SDT creates to some extent a dual set of WTO obligations between developed and developing countries that victimises many people in the world who are in search of the fullest economic measure of human flourishing. Yet, contrary to President Trump's tweeted assertion, the principal victims of the current approach to providing SDT in the WTO are not the United States and other developed countries. The main victims are the developing countries themselves; for, in the varied ways in which developing countries have been accorded such treatment for half a century and more, their path to full development has been blocked. By focusing on providing exemptions from WTO obligations instead of on providing the means for fulfilling all those obligations, the current approach to SDT has denied to many developing countries the assistance and the incentives they must have if they hope to achieve full development.

SDT gives developing country Members of the WTO greater flexibility than developed countries in meeting their WTO obligations. The WTO, however, has no agreed definition for what a developing country is, and as a result, Members practise self-declaration. They alone decide their development status. With developing countries worldwide at different stages of development, this use of SDT has created a situation where more advanced countries receive treatment similar to that accorded to countries that are much poorer. This similarity of treatment for countries at different levels of development undermines the initial rationale for SDT, which is to help those countries most in need with their transition to full compliance with all WTO obligations.

This is not a new complaint by the United States. American politicians of both parties have been making this complaint for nearly half a century. Nor is the United States alone among developed countries in complaining about SDT. To varying degrees involving varying sectors of trade, other developed countries feel much the same. Developed countries have long expressed concerns that developing countries are getting a "free ride" in the multilateral trading system, and that they should be made to comply with more WTO obligations more quickly. The supposed "free ride" given to developing countries through SDT has long been thought by developed countries to undermine the growth of trade and the overall health of the trading system. President Trump expressed this widely held view among developed countries in his memorandum instructing the United States Trade Representative on July 26, 2019 "When the wealthiest countries claim developing-country status, they harm not only other developed economies but also economies that truly require SDT. Such disregard for adherence to WTO rules, including the likely disregard of any future rules, cannot continue to go unchecked."[2]

At the same time, developing countries have long said that they are the ones disadvantaged by the structure of the world trading system. For nearly seven decades, developing countries have contended that it is in fact the United States and the other developed countries that are given an unfair advantage in the WTO trading system. They have long viewed this perceived disadvantage as due in no small part to what they see as the hollowness of their allotted SDT. Developing countries have consistently complained that they have not received all the benefits of the trade bargain they thought they had negotiated in the Uruguay Round trade agreements, which established the WTO in 1995. And, since the launch of the Doha Development Round of multilateral trade negotiations in 2001, they have lamented, time and again, about how WTO trade negotiators have failed to reach a consensus on a global furthering of additional "development" through trade.

These longstanding divisions between developed and developing countries over how developing countries should be treated in the WTO's rules-based trading system have been deepened by the transformation of the system since the establishment of the WTO. Since 1995, the WTO has grown by twenty-eight percent to 164 Members.[3] Almost all the new Members are developing countries, which now comprise a large majority of WTO membership. During that same time, there has been a substantial integration of the world economy and of world trade, which is increasingly conducted along inter-connected global supply chains and across digital lines of communication.

Adding tensions to the traditional differences between developed and developing countries over the nature and the legitimacy of SDT during that time has been the historic rise of several developing countries as serious economic rivals and competitors to the United States and other developed countries that have long gone unchallenged in the global economy. Since 2017, the exports of developing countries have represented almost half of all global exports. The largest 15 developing countries accounted for about three-fourths of those developing country exports.[4] The shape of the world economy is decidedly different from what it was in 1995.

Most of all, these divisions over SDT have deepened with the rise of China and with its increasingly significant role in the multilateral trading system. President Trump mentioned several countries in his memorandum to the United States Trade Representative, including Mexico, Turkey, South Korea, Singapore, Kuwait, the United Arab Emirates, and Qatar. But, of all the countries that continue to receive differential treatment due to their self-declared development status, Trump emphasised that "China most dramatically illustrates this point."[5] Increasingly an economic rival of the United States but steadfast in its assertion that it remains a developing country, China is by far the main source of the angst in the United States about the continuing grant of SDT to developing countries.

Hundreds of millions of Chinese have been lifted out of poverty since it opened to the wider world several decades ago. Poverty remains in China. Yet, China has reclaimed its historic role as a leader in the global economy. With its recent rise, China has become the leading exporter in the world, and its growth increasingly distinguishes it from many other developing countries. As Anabel González, a nonresident senior fellow at the Peterson Institute for International Economics and former senior director of the World Bank's global trade and competitiveness practice, has said of the worldwide economic transformation since the turn of the 21st century, there is "a strong rationale to have all larger economies abide by multilaterally agreed and applied disciplines because their policies affect international markets."[6]

The issue of providing SDT for Members of the WTO based on their different levels of development is an issue that is long overdue for serious attention in multilateral trade negotiations. With developed and developing countries alike firmly persuaded that they are being treated unfairly, there is an increasingly urgent need for achieving a consensus on a solution. Amid the current chaos afflicting the rules-based trading system, finding common ground on this divisive issue will surely be difficult to achieve. But finding it could lay the foundation for success in finding common ground also on other divisive trade issues that are impeding the progress of multilateral trade negotiations in the WTO.

In this book, we examine the landscape of SDT, and we reflect on possible avenues for compromise. The book begins with a look at a proposal by the United States in early 2019, which reignited the debate over this issue. We then turn to responses to the US proposal, from developing countries, and also from other developed countries, with emphasis on the arguments made against reform, and on the suggestions in these various proposals for how to bridge the divide. To give these perspectives a deeper context, we provide a historical overview of the evolution of SDT, highlighting the political environment under which the concept emerged and the lasting ambiguity over the outcomes it was meant to provide. Then, we evaluate whether SDT has lived up to the expectation that it would advance development. We conclude that the current approach has failed in this regard. In the next chapter, we pay particular attention to the complications created for the world trading system by the rise of China, and how these complications critically shape the debate over differentiation. Finally, we put forward an alternative approach to SDT, emphasising the need for a case-by-case, data-driven exercise in the grant of such treatment that should guide all future negotiations. In doing so, we argue that the heart of the compromise lies in committing to achieving sustainable development through the full inclusion of developing country Members within the WTO, and moving away from the practice of finding exemptions to the rules. We conclude with thoughts on the challenges that lie ahead, and on the unique opportunity recent debates have provided to reform SDT so that it will reflect the reality of the economic diversity of the WTO's membership, and will be better able to meet the specific needs of developing countries at their different stages of development.

Endnotes

1. Donald Trump (@realDonaldTrump), "The WTO is BROKEN when the world's RICHEST countries claim to be developing countries to avoid WTO rules and get special treatment. NO more!!! Today, I directed the U.S. Trade Representative to take action so that countries stop CHEATING the system at the expense of the USA!," Twitter, July 26, 2019, 11:29 a.m., https://twitter.com/realdonaldtrump/status/1154821023197474817?lang=en.
2. Presidential Memorandum for the United States Trade Representative, "Memorandum on Reforming Developing-Country Status in the World Trade Organization," (July 26, 2019), https://www.whitehouse.gov/presidential-actions/memorandum-reforming-developing-country-status-world-trade-organization/.
3. This figure varies based on how you count membership. If you look at GATT membership, there were 128 countries in 1994, but not all of those countries immediately signed on to the WTO agreements in 1995. If taking all GATT members into account, there has been a 28% increase since 1995. But if looking at WTO Membership in 1995, which stood at 112 Members, that would suggest growth in Membership of 46%.
4. Anabel González, "Bridging the Divide between Developed and Developing Countries in WTO Negotiations," Peterson Institute for International Economics Trade & Investment Policy Watch (March 12, 2019), https://www.piie.com/blogs/trade-investment-policy-watch/bridging-divide-between-developed-developing-countries-in-WTO-negotiations.
5. Presidential Memorandum for the United States Trade Representative, "Memorandum on Reforming Developing-Country Status in the World Trade Organization," July 26, 2019.
6. Anabel González, "Should Developing Countries Get Preferential Treatment on Trade?" Trade and Investment Policy Watch (August 27, 2019), https://www.piie.com/blogs/trade-and-investment-policy-watch/should-developing-countries-get-preferential-treatment-trade.

2 United States proposal on special and differential treatment

In February 2019, the United States circulated a proposal in the WTO calling for reform of special and differential treatment.[1] The US argued in this proposal that differential treatment has damaged the WTO's negotiating arm because it has been used in ways that are inconsistent with what the US sees as a foundational ambition of the WTO, concluding "reciprocal and mutually advantageous arrangements."[2] In a communication to all other WTO Members captioned "An Undifferentiated WTO: Self-Declared Development Status Risks Institutional Irrelevance," the United States makes three main assertions in support of its case for reform of differential treatment: first, that the world economy has fundamentally changed since the establishment of the WTO in 1995; second, that the act of "self-declaration" of developing country status is problematic and open to abuse; and third, that, because it lacks a precise definition, the WTO concept of "special and differential treatment" does not distinguish as it should between different stages of development.[3]

On the first of these assertions, the United States is right in pointing out that the world economy has fundamentally changed since 1995. In 2019, the World Bank estimated that there were 1.1 billion fewer people living in extreme poverty than in 1990, and that, from 1990–2015, the percentage of the global population living in poverty declined from 36 percent to 10 percent.[4] Regrettably, global poverty has risen again with the arrival of the Covid-19 pandemic in 2020. Yet, the incidence of poverty is still much less than what it was three decades ago. Since the establishment of the WTO, increased trade, in particular, has contributed to development by increasing economic opportunity and reducing poverty.[5] As more countries have reduced barriers to trade, the concentration of global trade has shifted. Where the United States, Europe, and Japan formerly held undisputed leadership in world trade, other countries, such as China, Singapore, South Korea, Brazil, Mexico, and India, have gradually grown in importance, and indeed have surpassed the traditional trade leaders in some respects.

According to the United States, though, this shift in the global economic landscape means little when the institution at the centre of the international trade regime does not even define what it means to be a developing country or specify what type of special and differential treatment should be accorded to developing countries. Except for least developed countries (LDCs) that are defined by the United Nations as countries that have human resource weakness, economic vulnerability, and a GNI per capita of less than $1,025,[6] the WTO does not distinguish between different levels of development, which the United States argues keeps the WTO "stuck in a simplistic and clearly outdated construct of 'North-South' division, developed and developing countries. Each is a seemingly static set, regardless of economic, social, trade, and other indicators."[7] This is a reasonable criticism of a system of trade treatment that has not been altered for about half a century, while the world economy has undergone enormous change.

On the second of its assertions, the United States warns that continuing to rely on self-declaration and failing to differentiate between and among WTO Members on the basis of their different levels of development has "put the WTO on a path to failed negotiations" as well as "institutional irrelevance."[8] Thus, in the US view, "the WTO remains anchored to the past and unable to negotiate disciplines to address the challenges of today or tomorrow, while other international institutions move forward."[9] The United States observes that although some self-declared "developing countries" view special and differential treatment as a transitional means to integrate fully and effectively over time into the multilateral trading system and ultimately "graduate" out of developing country status, others see such treatment as a way to escape from full compliance with WTO rules under the guise of maintaining space for discretionary domestic policymaking. As a result, when more-advanced developing countries demand the same flexibility as less-developed countries, it creates "asymmetries that ensure that ambition levels in WTO negotiations remain far too weak to sustain viable outcomes" in addition to diluting the benefits to LDCs and poorer countries.[10] Self-declaration, the United States claims, "has severely damaged the negotiating arm of the WTO by making differentiation among Members near impossible …[and] Members cannot find mutually agreeable trade-offs or build coalitions when significant players use self-declared development status to avoid making meaningful offers."[11]

On the third of its assertions, the US notes that the international practice of making distinctions between and among developing countries is not new. Other international institutions already make such distinctions and have for some time. They have used various criteria to differentiate between stages of development, including membership in the Organisation for Economic Co-operation and Development (OECD), the Human Development Index (HDI) of the United Nations Development Programme (UNDP), per capita income, and other income-based measures. The World Bank, for instance, customarily uses income classification by dividing countries on the basis of their gross national income (GNI) per capita into four classifications: low income ($995 or less), lower middle income ($996–$3895), upper middle income ($3896–$12,055), and high income ($12,056 and higher). These thresholds are adjusted annually. The United States is correct that the WTO can benefit from such categorical distinctions, because lumping countries that truly need help in the same category as those that do not risks harming the less-developed countries.

The United States argues that the absence of a formal definition in the WTO of a developing country or of other objective measures to identify which countries qualify for such status leads to abuse of the multilateral trading system. The United States notes that "[s]ome of the wealthiest WTO Members – including Singapore; Hong Kong, China; Macao, China; Israel; the State of Kuwait; the Republic of Korea; United Arab Emirates; Brunei Darussalam; and Qatar – insist on being considered developing Members and can avail themselves of differential treatment provisions at their discretion – just like Sub-Saharan Africa."[12] In practice, according to the US, this means that some countries are making fewer commitments and assuming less responsibility than they are able to do. For example, the United States points to the fact that one of the outcomes of the WTO Ministerial Conference in Bali in 2013 increased trade disciplines on protectionist actions that lead to unfilled tariff-rate quotas (TRQs), which restrict certain imports to a specific quantity at reduced-duty rates for a specified time period. But these new disciplines were applied only to developed country Members. Developing countries were excused. As the United States notes, this outcome in Bali "was the first time that Members agreed to use development status to exempt all self-declared developing Members from a new commitment rather than take a smaller cut or a longer time to implement."[13]

The United States maintains that this unwillingness to take on greater commitments on the part of advanced self-declared developing Members led to the collapse of the Doha Development Round, in which negotiations on non-agricultural market access became especially fraught. Although there was growth in the diversity of developing country groupings emerging at that time, the US claims that the advanced self-declared developing country Members took advantage of their developing country status to demand further flexibilities and carve-outs from the commitments. According to the United States, "Complex negotiating modalities and Members' unwillingness to differentiate poor developing Members from richer Members led to the collapse in agricultural negotiations. Negotiations simply could not keep pace with dramatic changes reshaping the global agricultural landscape."[14]

With these issues in mind, the United States has put forward a draft decision for consideration which states that WTO Members "will not avail themselves of special and differential treatment in current and future WTO negotiations" if they fit any of the following:

- are an OECD member or have begun the accession process to become one
- are a member of Group of 20 (G20) leading economies
- are classified as a "high income" country by the World Bank
- or account for 0.5 percent or more of global merchandise trade (imports and exports).[15]

The US proposal adds, "Nothing in this Decision precludes reaching agreement that in sector-specific negotiations other Members are also ineligible for special and differential treatment."[16] In effect, the proposed decision would amount to a definition of a developing country under WTO rules, with the possibility of expanding that definition in situations where countries that would otherwise be seen as developing countries have significant economic sway in particular sectors of trade (such as, for example, Brazil in soybeans and India in sugar).

More than 30 countries fall into one of these categories. Table 2.1 shows the countries that would meet at least one of these criteria.

10 *US proposal on special, differential treatment*

Table 2.1 Countries covered by U.S. proposal

Economy	OECD member	G20 member	World Bank high-income	Share in global merchandise trade
Antigua and Barbuda			x	0.00%
Argentina		x	x	0.35%
Bahrain			x	0.07%
Barbados			x	0.01%
Brazil		x		1.06%
Brunei Darussalam			x	0.03%
Chile	x		x	0.37%
China		x		11.58%
Colombia	x			0.25%
Costa Rica	x			0.07%
Hong Kong			x	3.23%
India		x		2.01%
Indonesia		x		0.89%
Israel	x		x	0.39%
Kuwait			x	0.25%
Macao			x	0.03%
Malaysia				1.13%
Mexico	x	x		2.37%
Oman			x	0.17%
Panama			x	0.10%
Qatar			x	0.29%
Saint Kitts and Nevis			x	0.00%
Saudi Arabia		x	x	1.04%
Seychelles			x	0.00%
Singapore			x	1.95%
South Africa		x		0.54%
South Korea	x	x	x	2.88%
Thailand				1.27%
Trinidad and Tobago			x	0.05%
Turkey	x	x		1.07%

Sources: "Member Countries," Organisation for Economic Co-operation and Development; "G20 Participants," G20; "World Bank Country and Lending Groups," World Bank; and "WTO Data Portal," World Trade Organization Data.

Note: Share in global merchandise trade calculated as the annual average from 2015 to 2017.

Endnotes

1. Draft General Council Decision, "Procedures to Strengthen the Negotiating Function of the WTO," submitted by the United States, WT/GC/W/764 (February 15, 2019).
2. Preamble, *Marrakesh Agreement Establishing the World Trade Organization.*
3. Communication from the United States, "An Undifferentiated WTO: Self-Declared Development Status Risks Institutional Irrelevance," WT/GC/W/757/Rev. 1 (February 14, 2019).
4. The World Bank, Understanding Poverty, Overview (updated April 3, 2019), https://www.worldbank.org/en/topic/poverty/overview.
5. "The Role of Trade in Ending Poverty," Joint Publication by the World Bank Group and the World Trade Organization (2015), https://www.wto.org/english/res_e/booksp_e/worldbankandwto15_e.pdf.
6. The WTO uses the United Nations' criteria for recognizing LDCs; see Article XI:2, WTO Agreement. See also, "LDC Identification Criteria & Indicators," United Nations Department of Economic and Social Affairs.
7. WT/GC/W/757/Rev.1, para. 1.5.
8. Ibid. at para. 5.2.
9. Ibid.
10. Ibid. at para. 4.5.
11. Ibid. at para. 4.5.
12. Ibid. at para. 4.4.
13. Ibid.
14. Ibid. at para. 4.10.
15. "Draft General Council Decision: Procedures to Strengthen the Negotiating Function of the WTO," World Trade Organization, WT/GC/W/764, February 15, 2019.
16. Ibid.

3 Responses to the United States proposal

Not surprisingly, the reforms proposed by the United States for granting special and differential treatment have been met with widespread opposition by the developing country Members of the WTO. Developing countries have not yielded an inch on their long-held view that the current approach to providing special and differential treatment is best for the world trading system. Their statements in defence of the current approach, however, do much to demarcate more fully their real division on the WTO's development dimension with the United States and other developed countries. At the same, some other developed countries, while echoing some of the US concerns, have tried to locate common ground where this divide may be narrowed through WTO negotiations.

Developing countries weigh in

Soon after the submission of the US proposal, ten developing countries, led by China, filed a communication in the WTO in which they did everything they could to refute it except mention the United States by name. Besides China, the developing countries that signed the communication included India, South Africa, Venezuela, Laos, Bolivia, Kenya, Cuba, Pakistan, and the Central African Republic. Notably absent were Brazil, South Korea, and Singapore, which have indicated bilaterally to the United States that they will forgo special and differential treatment in current and future WTO negotiations.[1] Also absent is Chinese Taipei – Taiwan – which has recently self-declared that it has become a developed country.[2]

As is often the case in criticisms made of other countries in the WTO, and has almost always been the case with comments by other WTO Members in opposition to the anti-WTO statements and actions of the Trump Administration, in their communication, these ten developing countries did not refer to the United States specifically. They referred only to "some Members" that are described as doubting what the developing countries portray as "the continued relevance of special and differential treatment in favour of developing Members and to promote development and ensure inclusiveness."[3] Yet, their communication amounts nevertheless to a reply brief to the US proposal.

In direct words that are rarely heard in the diplomatic circles of the WTO, China and the other nine developing countries argue that:

> recent attempts by some Members to selectively employ certain economic and trade data to deny the persistence of the divide between developing and developed Members, and to demand the former to abide by absolute "reciprocity" in the interest of "fairness" are profoundly disingenuous. The world has indeed changed in many ways since the GATT and the establishment of the WTO, but in overall terms the development divide remains firmly entrenched. It is therefore of greater concern that some Members would attempt to ignore this reality in an effort to deprive developing Members of their right to develop.[4]

China and the other nine developing countries maintain that special and differential treatment is one of the "cornerstone principles" of the WTO.[5] They insist that instances of such treatment are "not gifts" from developed countries but rather are rights that have been granted to developing countries by developed countries "through negotiations and compromises."[6] They also contend that the United States attempts to erase the dichotomy between developed and developing Members through specific economic indicators that gloss over the extent to which genuine development gaps remain. In contrast to the assertion of the United States, these developing countries claim that while "impressive progress [has been] achieved by some developing country Members since the creation of the WTO, old divides have not been substantially bridged and, in some areas they have even widened, while new divides, such as those in the digital and technological spheres, are becoming more pronounced."[7]

As these ten countries perceive it, "the status of developed and developing county Members" is not only "reflected in the bargaining process"; it is also "incorporated in the final rules themselves."[8] They see special and differential treatment for developing countries in the WTO, not merely as a practice, but also as "a fundamental right granted to all developing country Members."[9] Furthermore, in their view, "each developing Member shall, based upon its own particular situation, make the decision by itself on whether, when, where and how to use differential treatment, and to what extent as well."[10] To them, this approach "has proven to be the most appropriate to the WTO, which best serves the WTO objectives."[11]

As a further justification for their continued receipt of differential treatment, China and the nine other developing countries contend that domestic capacity constraints, such as the lack of human resources, negotiating capacity, and intra-governmental coordination, for example, "diminish not only the ability of developing Members to negotiate, but also the effectiveness of translating negotiated outcomes into measures for domestic economic growth."[12] These countries emphasise that "[T]he essence of development is the human being. Hence, per capita indicators must be given the top priority when assessing the development level of a country."[13] They cite as an example the mention of per capita indicators in the WTO subsidies rules.[14] They point to the still large gap between the GDP per capita of the United States and other developing countries, including even such advanced developing countries as China, India, Indonesia, and Brazil.[15] In countering the seeming US notion that some developing countries have in recent years attained something tantamount to developed status, China and the other nine countries note that the ten countries with the largest number of the world's poor and the largest number of the world's undernourished include China, India, Indonesia, and Pakistan.[16] Without question, there is merit in all of these observations.

Significantly, in stressing the human dimension of development, China and its nine co-signers endorse the broad view of development consistent with Nobel Prize winning economist Amartya Sen's concept of "development as freedom."[17] As they explain:

> Sen ... rejected the narrow argument of measuring growth only by means of GDP, and broadened the development measurement from promoting economic growth to "expanding people's capabilities". He argued that the ultimate goal of development should focus on the individual's freedom of choices, *i.e.* to improve the 'capabilities' of individuals to choose to live lives that they have reason to value.[18]

(It is noteworthy that China is advancing in an international institution the view that human freedom is defined by the ability to make free individual choices.)

Sen stresses the need to define "development" as "human development."[19] For him, "human freedom" is "the preeminent object of development," and the "[e]xpansion of freedom" is rightly viewed "both as the primary end and as the primary means of development."[20] He asserts that "Development consists of the removal of various types of unfreedoms that leave people with little choice and little opportunity of exercising their reasoned agency."[21] For Sen, human freedom is an individual act of choice made through the exercise of human reason and thus "[d]evelopment can be seen ... as a process of expanding the real freedoms that people enjoy" to make individual choices.[22] His novel capabilities approach to the measurement of development is not just a theoretical concept. It has been used for the past two decades as the philosophical underpinning for the annual Human Development Report of the United Nations Development Programme.[23] It can also be seen as the underlying philosophical foundation for the United Nations Sustainable Development Goals, which were agreed by all the members of the United Nations (including all the Members of the WTO) in 2015 and which comprise the United Nations Agenda for 2030.[24]

In their reply to the United States, China and the nine other developing countries provide an intellectual justification for special and differential treatment to support their view that development status should continue to be self-declared and that self-declared developing countries should continue to be allowed to comply gradually with WTO disciplines. But, their proposals do not clearly explain how the status quo serves to improve human capabilities, the central component of Sen's thesis. Instead, they claim that developing countries need "policy space when opening up to the global market to push forward their domestic reform and transformation agenda, which is exactly the reason why the WTO adopts the self-declaration approach."[25] Yet, "policy space" is a vague term that can be understood as a blank check permitting developing countries to decide when, if ever, they will assume additional trade obligations. Furthermore, their proposals identify no clear pathway developing countries should take towards graduation to full compliance with WTO obligations.

This is also a broad reading of what the concept of less than full "reciprocity" means in the context of special and differential treatment. The Enabling Clause adopted in 1979 that permits trade discrimination for the purpose of providing SDT to developing countries states that developing countries should not be required to make "concessions that are inconsistent with the latter's development, financial and trade needs."[26] But, in no way does the Enabling Clause cite a need for policy space as a reason for excusing developing countries from complying with the same WTO obligations that bind developed countries.

However, an area where China and others have levelled an important critique is in agriculture. Agriculture continues to be a main source of employment for individuals in developing countries, whereas overall agricultural employment in developed countries has declined significantly. One reason for the decline in developed country employment has been the growth of automation in this sector, which has enormously boosted productivity per worker. Developed countries, however, also disproportionately subsidise their agricultural industries relative to the size of the industry in their domestic markets. These subsidies provided by developed countries for their own agricultural products distort agricultural trade in their own markets and also in world markets to the great disadvantage of the agricultural products of developing countries, which are denied what should be the benefits of their comparative advantage in agricultural trade. The proposal points out that developed WTO Members account for more than 90 percent of the global entitlements for Aggregate Measures of Support (AMS), which are price supports governments are allowed to apply to specific product categories without violating WTO rules. This has been a repeated refrain of developing countries since the very beginning of the multilateral trading system. Developing countries with a comparative advantage in agricultural trade point quite rightly to the farm trade distortions caused by developed countries through their many quantitative restrictions on agricultural imports and their domestic price-support measures that subsidise trade in their own agricultural products. Because many developing countries continue to rely mainly on agricultural exports, this is a critical issue for them. Long on the trade agenda, liberalisation of agricultural trade is long overdue.[27] Liberalising trade in agriculture would do much to accelerate the economic advance of developing countries and would do much to address the coming crisis in food supply predicted by climate scientists.[28]

Finally, China and the other nine countries also point to the process within the WTO that has supposedly been working on ways to improve SDT by making it "more precise, effective and operational" since the launch of the Doha Development Round in 2001.[29] In reality, though, little has been achieved through this process. In 2013, an SDT monitoring mechanism was established as a special session within the WTO Committee on Trade and Development; but, as of the tenth session of this monitoring mechanism, held in January 2019, not a single written submission had been put forward by any WTO Member, including developing countries. If special and differential treatment needs reform, there has, until now, been scant evidence of any appetite to take action to reform it.

The exception that stands out is the United States. President Trump's tweet in July 2019 was only a blunt and blustery escalation of what has long been the prevailing bipartisan US sentiment on providing developing countries with special and differential treatment. More than 14 years before Trump was elected President, at the regular meeting of the WTO Committee on Trade and Development in June 2002, the United States expressed essentially the same view when observing that "[t]here seems to be a difference of view among Members. Some appear to view differential treatment as an end in itself, while others perceive differential treatment as one of several tools to foster economic development, adjustment, and integration into the multilateral trading system."[30]

In a separate communication,[31] Bolivia, Cuba, Ecuador, India, Oman, and the African Members of the WTO express similar concerns but, notably, place their developmental ambitions within the context of the UN Sustainable Development Goals, saying, "The SDGs articulate important development challenges still confronting developing countries, including overcoming poverty and hunger. WTO rules must be supportive, rather than a constraint to these efforts."[32] While the countries that signed this communication are firm in their defence of differential treatment, describing it as a "treaty-embedded and non-negotiable right for all developing Members," they all acknowledge that SDT is not an end in itself. In fact, in criticising calls by the United States and other developed countries for enhanced transparency obligations, they state that their "non-compliance is not willful" but is rather a matter of not having sufficient capacity to ensure compliance.[33] Implicitly, these developing countries seem to be signalling that they would be willing to assume additional WTO obligations if they had the sufficient capacity to do so and if developed countries were willing to help provide them with the resources, the technology, and the know-how they lack.

This communication provides further evidence of the need for greater differentiation between developing countries to ensure that those countries that need help are the ones that receive it. In addition, the fact that China was not a signatory to this proposal suggests that others may not share entirely China's dismissive attitude towards reform of SDT. These voices should not be drowned out of reform efforts and are essential to bridging the gap between developed and developing country Members in building the required consensus for change.

Other developed countries push for balance and pragmatism

In addition to the United States, other developed countries have contributed to the emerging debate with their own suggestions for pragmatic approaches to bridge the current divide over the development dimension in the WTO. Norway submitted a communication on April 26, 2019, calling for a "constructive conversation" about "the development dimension."[34] The Norwegian communication has since been endorsed by Canada, Hong Kong, Iceland, Mexico, New Zealand, Singapore, and Switzerland. In contemplating the "polarized views" of WTO Members on the issue of differential treatment, Norway advises:

> Our ability to achieve multilateral outcomes would be significantly enhanced by a more solution-oriented approach to the issue of trade and development. Furthermore, by improving the chances of success in our rule-making efforts, a more pragmatic approach to differential treatment is also an important element in the broader efforts to safeguard and strengthen the multilateral, rules-based trading system.[35]

In what seems a critique of the crux of the US proposal, Norway disagrees about the efficacy of using eligibility requirements and concludes that "consensus on a negotiated set of criteria for when a developing Member should have access to S&D is neither realistic nor necessarily useful," but that "[t]he question should rather be how S&D could be designed to address the developing challenges Members are facing. It is the negotiated result that matters, not the categorization of Members."[36] (Norway is, however, quick to add that "the special treatment of LDCs should be maintained.")[37]

The Norwegians submit in their communication that "S&D is not a single, clearly defined and operational modality," and as a result, the binary approach, focusing on Members as developed or developing, is not useful.[38] They argue:

> To focus on the status of Members in binary terms – as either developed or developing – complicates the search for an appropriate balance of rights and obligations. It also hampers the effectiveness of S&D as an enabler of development through trade and as a means of ensuring balanced and inclusive participation in multilateral negotiations.[39]

Instead, the Norwegians favour "[i]mplementing our shared commitment to S&D in a more flexible and effective way ...."[40] They recommend that the Members of the WTO seek alternative pathways to reach their common objectives as set out in the WTO agreements. Furthermore, they maintain that these pathways can be tailored to fit particular needs in particular situations.

In elaborating, Norway insists, "The tools already exist for a creative and effective approach to flexibilities that respond to the development needs of Members" in fulfillment of common objectives of all Members of the WTO.[41] For example, the Norwegians point to how the WTO Agreement on Technical Barriers to Trade (TBT) and the WTO General Agreement on Trade in Services (GATS) have established "minimum baseline approaches" to both setting and managing standards.[42] A common starting point, Norway states, can help facilitate the acceptance of greater commitments by developing countries over time.

Pointing to the WTO Trade Facilitation Agreement (TFA) concluded at the Ministerial Conference in Bali, Indonesia, in 2013, Norway notes how this latest multilateral trade agreement allows developing countries to pick their own path towards implementation of their obligations. Under the TFA, developing Members are able to schedule their own commitments by choosing whether to be included in one of three separate categories: in the first, implementation of all obligations is immediate; in the second, obligations are phased in over a specified period of time; while, in the third, obligations are conditioned on the receipt by the developing country of technical assistance.[43] The TFA is a departure from past WTO agreements in that signatories have self-identified specific short- and long-term implementation timelines, and have also identified those provisions for which their implementation will require technical assistance. This approach is novel in that it links SDT to an identified need, as opposed to a general opt-out on certain commitments.

Canada voiced similar sentiments in a communication to other WTO Members on September 24, 2018, which broadly addresses a number of aspects for potential WTO reform.[44] Much like Norway, Canada advises that a new approach to the development dimension is needed that strikes a balance between reciprocity and flexibility. The Canadians argue that "not all countries need or should benefit from the same level of flexibility," and they suggest, again like Norway, that the TFA is a good example of how SDT should be approached in the future.[45] In particular, Canada notes that the following considerations may inform a new approach: while transitional periods may be necessary, the long-term goal should be convergence and full implementation; differentiated treatment should be based on evidence of need; and the most onerous obligations, at least for those countries with the least capacity, should be linked with capacity building supported by developed countries.[46]

In addition, the European Union released a concept paper on WTO reform on September 18, 2018, which includes its suggestions for reform of SDT.[47] The EU agrees with the United States that some developing Members are better placed to assume more obligations than others. To address this gap in capacity, the EU offers three suggestions. First, it proposes that developing countries should be encouraged to "graduate" from special and differential treatment, and that, when electing to employ such treatment, they should explain how they intend to use it to advance their development and also provide a target date for when they will fully assume all WTO obligations.[48] This topic, the EU adds, could become a part of the WTO process of regular reviews of the trade policies of all WTO Members, with the four Members that make up a larger share of world trade, like China, reviewed more frequently.[49] Second, the EU states that, for future agreements, differential treatment should be both needs-driven and evidence-based, meaning that, as a starting point, all parties should acknowledge universal implementation as the goal, that added commitments require flexibility, and that flexibility be proportional to the number of Members party to the agreement in question. Third, and lastly, although the EU maintains that the existing provisions for differential treatment should not be changed, it recommends that any requests for additional special and differential treatment should require the specification of a clearly identified development objective; an economic analysis of the measure's impact, including an analysis of its impact on other WTO Members because the obligation has not been met; and a specified time period for which the developing country will need flexibility.[50]

Endnotes

1. Joint Statement from President Donald J. Trump and President Jair Bolsonaro, The White House, March 19, 2019, https://www.whitehouse.gov/briefings-statements/joint-statement-president-donald-j-trump-president-jair-bolsonaro/; Jane Chung and Joori Roh, "South Korea to give up developing country status in WTO talks," *Reuters* (October 24, 2019), https://www.reuters.com/article/us-southkorea-trade-wto/south-korea-to-give-up-developing-country-status-in-wto-talks-idUSKBN1X401W; Statement delivered by Dennis Shea, Deputy United States Trade Representative and Ambassador to the World Trade

Organization, Davos, Switzerland (January 24, 2020), https://geneva.usmission.gov/2020/01/27/statement-by-ambassador-shea-at-davos-informal-wto-ministerial-gathering/.
2. Kensaku Ihuara, "Taiwan quits 'developing economy' status in WTO with eye on China," *Nekkei Asia Review* (October 17, 2018), at https://asia.nikkei.com/Politics/Taiwan-quits-developing-economy-status-in-WTO-with-eye-on-China.
3. "The Continued Relevance of Special and Differential Treatment in Favour of Developing Members to Promote Development and Ensure Inclusiveness," WT/GC/W/765/Rev. 2 (4 March 2019) para. 1.2.
4. Ibid. at para. 1.2.
5. Ibid. at para 1.4.
6. Ibid. at para. 1.5.
7. Ibid. at para. 1.1.
8. Ibid. at para. 1.7.
9. Ibid. at para. 6.2.
10. Ibid.
11. Ibid. at para. 1.7.
12. Ibid. at 1.3.
13. Ibid. at para. 2.3.
14. Article 8.2 (b)(iii), WTO Agreement on Subsidies and Countervailing Measures.
15. WT/GC/W/765/Rev. 2, at para. 2.4.
16. Ibid. at paras. 2.5 and 2.6.
17. Amartya Sen, *Development as Freedom* (New York: Random House, 1999).
18. WT/GC/W/765/Rev. 2, at para. 3.1.
19. For a discussion of Sen's view of "development as freedom," *see* James Bacchus, *The Willing World: Shaping and Sharing a Sustainable Global Prosperity* (Cambridge, UK: Cambridge University Press, 2018), 17–18.
20. Amartya Sen, *Development as Freedom*, at xii.
21. Ibid.
22. Ibid. at 3.
23. *See* United Nations Human Development Reports, at http://www.hdr.undp.org/en/global-reports.
24. "Transforming Our World: The 2030 Agenda for Sustainable Development," A/RES/70/1 (September 25, 2015).
25. WT/GC/W/765/Rev.2, at para. 5.14.
26. Differential and More Favourable Treatment Reciprocity and Fuller Participation of Developing Countries, Decision of November 28, 1979 (L/4903), commonly referred to as the "Enabling Clause."
27. Daniel Griswold, Stephen Slivinski, and Christopher A. Preble, "Ripe for Reform: Six Good Reasons to Reduce U.S. Farm Subsidies and Trade Barriers," *Trade Policy Analysis No.30* (September 14, 2005), at https://www.cato.org/publications/trade-policy-analysis/ripe-reform-six-good-reasons-reduce-us-farm-subsidies-trade-barriers.
28. The Intergovernmental Panel on Climate Change (IPCC), "Climate Change and Land: an IPCC special report on climate change, desertification, land degradation, sustainable land management, food security,

and greenhouse gas fluxes in terrestrial ecosystems," (August 8, 2019), at https://www.ipcc.ch/srccl-report-download-page/.
29. Doha Ministerial Declaration, WT/MIN(01)/DEC/1 (adopted November 14, 2001).
30. WTO Committee on Trade and Development, Special Session, TN/CTD/W/9 (June 28, 2002) para. 6.
31. "Strengthening the WTO to Promote Development and Inclusivity," Communication from Plurinational State of Bolivia, Cuba, Ecuador, India, Malawi, Oman, South Africa, Tunisia, Uganda, and Zimbabwe WT/GC/W/778/Rev.1 (July 22, 2019). An updated version, WT/GC/W/778/Rev.2 (August 7, 2019) includes the African Group (which consists of all African WTO members).
32. WT/GC/W/778/Rev.2, at para. 4.5.
33. This issue was also mentioned by the African Group, Cuba, India, and Oman, which also called for greater transparency in developed country notifications. *See* "An Inclusive Approach to Transparency and Notification Requirements in the WTO," JOB/GC/218/Rev.2 (26 July 2019).
34. "Pursuing the Development Dimension in WTO Rule-Making Efforts," Communication from Norway; Canada; Hong Kong, China; Iceland; Mexico; New Zealand; Singapore; and Switzerland, WT/GC/W/770/Rev.3 (April 26, 2019), para. 1.3.
35. Ibid. at para. 1.2.
36. Ibid. at para. 4.2.
37. Ibid.
38. Ibid. at para. 2.2.
39. Ibid. at para. 2.3.
40. Ibid. at para. 4.4.
41. Ibid. at para. 4.3.
42. Ibid. at paras. 3.7 and 3.8.
43. Trade Facilitation Agreement, Article 14: Categories of Provisions, WT/L/940 (November 28, 2014).
44. "Strengthening and Modernizing the WTO: Discussion Paper," Communication from Canada, JOB/GC/201 (September 24, 2018).
45. Ibid. at 5–6.
46. Ibid. at 6.
47. European Commission for Trade, WTO Modernisation: Introduction to Future EU Proposals (European Union 2018), http://trade.ec.europa.eu/doclib/docs/2018/september/tradoc_157331.pdf.
48. World Trade Organization, Trade Policy Review Mechanism, at https://www.wto.org/english/docs_e/legal_e/29-tprm_e.htm.
49. World Trade Organization, Trade Policy Review Mechanism, https://www.wto.org/english/docs_e/legal_e/29-tprm_e.htm.
50. European Commission for Trade, WTO Modernisation: Introduction to Future EU Proposals (European Union 2018), http://trade.ec.europa.eu/doclib/docs/2018/september/tradoc_157331.pdf.

4 The evolution of differential treatment

The development dimension has been a part of the now WTO-based multilateral trading system since the General Agreement on Tariffs and Trade (the GATT) was agreed by the 23 original "Contracting Parties" in 1947.[1] The GATT was not the construct of the developed world alone. Ten of the original 23 GATT Contracting Parties could have been classified at the time as developing countries, including (pre-communist) China.[2] Nevertheless, as Frank Garcia has aptly put it, "In the beginning, there was no special and differential treatment."[3] Before the GATT negotiations began in 1946, in the immediate aftermath of the devastating destruction of the Second World War, there had never been any mention of special and differential treatment in any previous international trade agreement.[4] Nor was there any mention of SDT in the eventual agreed text of the GATT. Indeed, the original GATT made no formal distinction between developed and developing countries.

In part, this initial textual absence can be attributed to the underlying assumption in trade negotiations (which prevailed then as now) that a decision by one country to lower its tariffs or other trade barriers to the goods or services of another country is a "concession" to that other country. Almost all economists will be quick to point out that this is a political and not an economic assumption. It is based on the fundamental fallacy that opening one's market is a "concession" that needs to be "paid" for – that tariffs and other barriers to imports are national assets that should be relinquished only in exchange for improved market access abroad.[5] Economically, this makes no sense. Indeed, quite the opposite is true. It makes perfect sense, economically, for a country to reduce its barriers to trade with other countries – whether those other countries, in return, reduce their barriers to its trade or not. A country generally benefits from reducing its barriers to trade with other countries, regardless of what those other countries do.

Unilateral trade liberalisation creates domestic economic gains. But, such sensible action is little understood by voters (or, alas, all too many politicians) in every part of the world.

Thus, except in the smallest countries and in city-states such as Singapore, which depend much more than other states on the constant inflow and outflow of trade, it is exceedingly difficult almost everywhere for politicians to reduce trade barriers unilaterally. For the most part, domestic politics dictates that most countries can summon the political support to liberalise trade only if other countries do so at the same time – only bilaterally or multilaterally. For this reason, when aspiring to further trade liberalisation, in return for cutting a tariff or lowering another barrier to trade, almost all international trade negotiators require a comparable trade "concession" that they can showcase to domestic constituents back home as evidence that, despite the "concession," they gained overall from the trade deal.

Still underlying trade negotiations today, this agreed architecture of multilateral trade negotiations is called "reciprocity." A trade agreement is seen as "reciprocal" if every country that has negotiated the agreement believes that the agreement contains a "balance of concessions" – that the "concessions" it has obtained through the agreement match the "concessions" it has made. (Note that, in focusing on an *overall* balance of concessions in *all traded products*, "reciprocity" in trade does not mean what many in the Trump Administration and in the Congress of the United States think it means; it does not mean a balance of concessions *product for product*.)[6]

In adherence with this principle of reciprocity, generally, all countries were treated equally in the give and take of the first several postwar GATT rounds of multilateral trade negotiations, which focused mainly on liberalising trade by lowering tariffs. But, of course, in their stages of development, all countries were far from equal. In the first few decades following the Second World War, the United States, emerging economically unscathed and fully mobilised from the global conflict, was by far the leading force in the global economy. The economies of Europe and Japan gradually recovered (thanks in no small part to the generosity of the United States). The Soviet Union gradually recovered, and it seemed throughout the Cold War largely to persist, the mounting signs of its eventual collapse mostly visible only now in retrospective aftermath. Meanwhile, the poorer countries of the world, including dozens of the newly independent countries freed from colonialism, at first comprised together only a small slice of the global economy.

One by one, many of these poorer countries, often with the sponsorship of their former colonisers, joined the GATT. Although often on the margins, these countries struggling to climb up the steep ladder of development nevertheless became a part of the growing multilateral trading system. At first, they were outnumbered by the United States and other developed countries. But, gradually, their numbers grew, and, before the first decade of the GATT had passed, developing countries succeeded in exacting from the developed countries two changes in the GATT that for the first time instilled the concept of special and differential treatment for developing countries as an obligation of the multilateral trading system.

In 1955, beseeched by the growing number of poorer and post-colonial countries in the new trading system, the contracting parties to the GATT adopted a substantial revision of GATT Article XVIII, which was rewritten to give clear authorisation to developing countries to enact measures to protect infant industries and to afford them additional ease in imposing trade restrictions when facing balance of payments difficulties.[7] At the same time, the GATT contracting parties introduced GATT Article XXVIII *bis*, which formally introduced the concept of "non-reciprocity" into the legal text. It did so by stating that, henceforth, multilateral trade negotiations should take into account "the needs of less-developed countries for a more flexible use of tariff protection to assist their economic development and the special needs of these countries to maintain tariffs for revenue purposes; and...all other relevant circumstances, including the fiscal, developmental, strategic and other needs of the contracting parties concerned."[8] With this change in the GATT, the original rigid adherence of the multilateral trading system to the concept of "reciprocity" was relaxed, and its previously implicit distinction between developed and developing countries in the trading system became more explicit.

But, which were the countries entitled to special and differential treatment? Because no textual distinction had been made originally in the GATT between developed and developing countries, there was no need in 1947 for a definition of a developing country. The changes made in 1955 also did not provide one. Thus, there was no need for any country to fit within an agreed definition of a developing country when claiming to be one. It was therefore left to each country in the trading system to choose for itself whether it wished to be treated as a developing country within the multilateral trading system. The process of identification became (and remains) one of self-selection in which self-anointed "developing countries" justify their status simply by announcing it.

One aspect of the development dimension on which all countries have agreed from the beginning is that least developed countries

(LDCs) must be treated differently and therefore are not expected to provide reciprocity in trade agreements. The WTO recognises LDCs that have been designated as such by the United Nations if it is determined to have human resource weakness, economic vulnerability, and a gross national income per capita of less than US $1025.[9] There are 47 such countries on the UN list.[10] To date, 36 of these countries have become WTO Members. Largely, they are small island states and countries in sub-Saharan Africa. The persistence of poverty – despite the growth of trade and other advances in the global economy during the past generation – is evidenced by the fact that only six LDCs have graduated from the UN list since the conclusion of the Uruguay Round trade agreements establishing the WTO in 1994.

Yet, for all those countries that are not LDCs but that nevertheless claim developing country status, the practice of self-selection has prevailed. Subsequent elaborations in the trade rules have given a semblance of additional substance to such status, but all such elaborations have stopped short of supplying an actual definition of what a developing country is. Accordingly, there is, to this day, nothing remotely approaching a consensus in the trading system on the meaning of a developing country or on the criteria that should be employed in identifying one.

By the 1960s, developing countries comprised most of the Contracting Parties to the GATT, and they sought more legal content for their developing status in the trading system. Desirous of additional special and differential treatment, they used their newfound majority as negotiating leverage to secure the adoption of Part IV of the GATT, on "Trade and Development," which took effect in 1966. Part IV added three Articles – XXXVI, XXXVII, and XXXVIII – to the GATT. Most notable by far in this provision is Article XXXVI:8, which recognises the notion of "non-reciprocity," stating that "The developed country parties do not expect reciprocity for commitments made by them in trade negotiations to reduce or remove tariffs and other barriers to the trade of less-developed contracting parties."[11]

Part IV of the GATT is replete with exhortatory language. Article XXXVI acknowledges the need for better trading opportunities for developing countries.[12] Article XXXVII includes undertakings by developed countries to provide better access for developing countries to their markets.[13] Article XXXVIII features commitments for joint action and support to promote development through trade.[14] But all this language is *only* exhortatory – "The adoption of measures to give effect to these principles and objectives shall be a matter of conscious and purposeful effort" by developed countries.[15] It is not, however, mandatory. It is not legally binding. Thus, these obligations are not enforceable by developing countries against developed countries in WTO dispute settlement. The fact that these three articles of Part IV of the GATT have no legal force has "led to resentment among developing countries" and hardened the division over development in the trading system.[16]

With developed countries still firmly committed to an ultimate goal of reciprocity and with developing countries equally committed to non-reciprocity, multilateral trade negotiations in the succeeding decades gradually became, for almost all countries, and for developing countries especially, more and more a matter of seeing how little they could *give* in trade concessions in exchange for what they *got*. Because they were no longer facing demands from developed countries for full reciprocity, often, developing countries gave little. As a result, they did not get much more than they gave. Through the operation of non-reciprocity, the seeds were sown for that sense of being unfairly treated within the trading system that today grips developed and developing countries alike. Both are persuaded that they are giving too much and getting too little under the multilateral rules of trade.

Along the way, additional efforts have been made to afford more substantial privileges to those countries with developing country status. In 1971, the GATT approved the establishment, for 10 years, of trade preferences for developing countries that would otherwise have violated the basic obligation of "most favoured nation" treatment, which forbids trade discrimination between and among imported like products.[17] This preferential arrangement is known as the Generalized System of Preferences – or, commonly, GSP. Between 1971 and 1976, about twenty developed countries, including the United States, implemented GSP preferences for developing countries. In 1979, GSP approval was extended permanently through the adoption by the GATT Contracting Parties of the so-called "Enabling Clause," which permits developed countries to adopt discriminatory tariff arrangements that favour imports from developing countries.[18]

It was in the 1970s that the United States also first began to express the antecedents of the view on differential treatment later given voice by President Trump. This was about the same time when products of developing countries first began to compete with those of the United States in the US and other global markets. In response to this economic challenge, the United States began "insisting that at some stage some of the developing countries should 'graduate' and be counted among the developed contracting parties" of the GATT.[19] Confronted by mounting domestic resistance to giving developing countries SDT, and continuing to hold economic reservations about the efficacy of such treatment, developed countries often undermined GSP privileges even as they granted them. Usually omitted from GSP preferences were the labour-intensive, and therefore politically sensitive, products in which developing countries could have been the most competitive in the domestic markets of developed countries. Furthermore, GSP treatment was discretionary and therefore less than certain, which undermined salutary investments by developing countries in the production of GSP-traded products.

In addition, in what amounted to reverse discrimination, developed countries began to impose quotas, voluntary export restraints, and other forms of managed trade to protect their domestic producers from competition from the products of developing countries in sectors in which developing countries enjoy a comparative advantage and could benefit significantly from freer access to the domestic markets of developing countries. Most notably, these protectionist arrangements limited the trade of developing countries in textiles, clothing, footwear, and agriculture. Through trade actions such as these, developed countries implied to developing countries that their support for differential treatment was "only a political gesture."[20]

Questions surrounding the development dimension were much on display throughout the 8 years of the Uruguay Round of multilateral trade negotiations that concluded in 1994 with the Marrakesh Agreement establishing the World Trade Organization.[21] The Uruguay Round trade agreements were a single undertaking in which each of the negotiating countries, developed and developing alike, was required to agree to every one of the seventeen multilateral agreements in order to benefit from any of them. This requirement amounted to a movement away from non-reciprocity that many developing countries resented at the time and still resent now. Yet, diminishing the extent of this resentment was the fact that, while developing countries had to be bound by all of the multilateral agreements, there were provisions in many of those agreements that promised special and differential treatment to developing countries.

The WTO Secretariat has listed 183 provisions for special and differential treatment contained in the WTO covered agreements – a sum which does not include the additional subsequent provisions for such treatment found in the decisions of the WTO Ministerial Conference and the WTO Council and in the new Trade Facilitation Agreement.[22] Some of these numerous provisions for SDT provide flexibility for developing countries in the fulfillment of their trade obligations and in the domestic measures and other actions they take. Some are simply "best endeavor" undertakings that lack any binding legal force.

Others provide transitional periods for phasing in WTO legal obligations. Still, others relate to delivery of technical assistance to developing countries by developed countries. And a number are special provisions exclusively for LDCs.

For his part, Garcia perceives the emphasis on transitional periods in the Uruguay Round trade agreement as especially telling. He sees a pivotal change in the provision of special and differential treatment in those agreements, which he describes in the following way:

> [A]lthough the Uruguay Round agreements retained many S&D elements, these provisions as a whole ... reveal a fundamental shift away from traditional nonreciprocity. Instead of maintaining full nonreciprocity of obligation, the system shifted to limited nonreciprocity of obligation. Developing countries lost the option of maintaining different levels of obligation and instead were granted additional periods of time to *adjust* to the burdens of fully-implemented WTO obligations.[23]

Thus, the focus in providing special and differential treatment in the Uruguay Round trade agreements shifted from having a different level of trade obligations for developing countries to giving those countries an agreed period of time to adjust to full compliance with WTO rules.

Since the transformation of the GATT into the WTO in 1995, and despite the long list of agreed provisions for SDT in the WTO covered agreements, developing countries have complained repeatedly that they have not gotten the benefit of the bargain they thought they had struck with developed countries in the Uruguay Round. The Uruguay Round trade agreements abolished many of the restrictions imposed by developed countries on imports of textiles and clothing; but numerous other restrictions to access to developed country markets for many of the principal manufactured products of developing countries remain. The Uruguay Round trade agreements also set the stage for liberalising more trade in developing country agricultural products. In a noteworthy achievement, farm export subsidies were abolished at the WTO ministerial conference in Nairobi in 2015, but hopes for additional access for agricultural products to the markets of developed countries remain largely unfulfilled. Moreover, many developing countries lament that, even if they did get all they thought they had in the Uruguay Round, it is not enough. With so many developing countries still falling far short of what they envisage as the full extent of their development, they feel they are due additional dispensations in the WTO trade rules as they try to come to terms with the ineluctable forces of an ever-encroaching economic globalisation.

30 *The evolution of differential treatment*

Soon after the September 11 terrorist attacks in 2001, the Members of the WTO gathered in Doha, Qatar, to launch what they named the "Doha Development Round" of multilateral trade negotiations, the first full round of negotiations since the establishment of the WTO 6 years earlier. In the shadow of a lethal terrorism spawned in part by the widening chasms in the world between prosperity and deprivation, and hope and despair, a clearly stated aim of the Doha round was to promote development.[24] By consensus, the Members of the WTO stated:

> Recalling the Preamble to the Marrakesh Agreement (establishing the WTO), we shall continue to make positive efforts designed to ensure that developing countries, and especially the least-developed among them, secure a share in the growth of world trade commensurate with the needs of their economic development. In this context, enhanced market access, balanced rules, and well targeted, sustainably financed technical assistance and capacity-building programmes have important roles to play.[25]

Several specific mandates were set out in the Ministerial Declaration on the Doha Development Round and in the accompanying Decision on Implementation-Related Issues and Concerns[26] to achieve this aim in the Doha Development Agenda. These Doha mandates included many developing Members' long sought after commitments including: examining issues related to trade and technology transfer to increase flows of technology to developing countries[27]; ensuring that technical assistance and capacity-building programmes are designed to assist LDCs and other developing countries in adjusting to WTO rules[28]; committing to the objective of duty-free, quota-free access for products originating from LDCs and considering additional measures for progressive improvements in market access for LDCs[29]; and, significantly, reviewing all special and differential treatment provisions in WTO rules which give developing countries special rights so as to strengthen them and make them more precise.[30]

Developing countries thought the review of their special rights mandated by the Doha Declaration would lead to more, and to more extensive, special treaty rights through an enhanced form of special and differential treatment. From the outset, though, it was not at all clear that developed countries shared this view. No single country or group of countries was to blame for the ultimate collapse of the Doha round. There were many reasons for its ultimate failure, such as the intransigence of the European Union and the United States on reducing their agricultural subsidies that frustrate the competitive agricultural trade of many developing countries; the refusal of China, India, and other developing countries to open up their markets to more of the manufactured products and the services of developed countries; and much more. There is blame aplenty to go around.

This did, however, highlight that one of the main obstacles to success in the negotiations was the development dimension. The utter lack of anything approaching a consensus among 164 developed and developing countries over the meaning of the mandate in Paragraph 44 of the Doha Declaration to review all special and differential treatment provisions was one of the principal and pervasive reasons for the collapse. This lack of consensus on SDT contributed much to the prolonged negotiating stalemate and to the de facto demise of the ill-fated round in Nairobi in 2015.[31] The Doha round was a huge missed opportunity for all WTO Members. In failing to forge a consensus to fulfill the Doha Development Agenda, WTO Members failed also to make any progress on advancing the development of its poorer Members. In the aftermath of these failures, the issue of special and differential treatment has become even more divisive.

Ordinarily, WTO Members might look to the WTO's formal avenues for dispute settlement to clarify their mutual obligations. But on this issue, in the absence of a definition of SDT in the legal text of the WTO covered agreements, WTO panels and the WTO Appellate Body have not been able to clarify the distinction between developed and developing countries. Jurists in WTO trade disputes have rightly assumed under the current rules that WTO Members are developing countries when they say they are. Nor has there been any clarification in 25 years of WTO dispute settlement of how, if at all, the concept of special and differential treatment should apply to specific WTO obligations. The limited case law has mainly dealt with the details of GSP treatment under the Enabling Clause.[32]

Despite the assertions of some developing countries in WTO dispute settlement and elsewhere, as a matter of WTO law, there is no all-pervasive concept of special and differential treatment that somehow permeates all WTO obligations and therefore colours how they are to be clarified in the light of such treatment. In the absence of any definitive guidance from the negotiators of the WTO Agreement as to a general meaning for special and differential treatment in the legal text, the adoption in WTO dispute settlement of an interpretive approach that embraced such an overarching legal concept would lead inevitably to the addition and/or the subtraction of the rights and obligations provided in the covered agreements, which is clearly prohibited by the agreed dispute settlement rules.[33] Instead, in WTO dispute settlement, special and differential treatment exists only if it is required by a specific WTO obligation, and then only to the extent that it is specified in that obligation. Thus, the issue has been left to further negotiations.

Endnotes

1. The 23 founding members were: Australia, Belgium, Brazil, Burma, Canada, Ceylon, Chile, China, Cuba, Czechoslovakia, France, India, Lebanon, Luxembourg, Netherlands, New Zealand, Norway, Pakistan, Southern Rhodesia, Syria, South Africa, United Kingdom, and the United States.
2. Michael Hart and Bill Dymond, "Special and Differential Treatment and the Doha 'Development' Round," *Journal of World Trade*, Vol. 37, No. 2 (2003): 395, 399.
3. Frank J. Garcia, "Beyond Special and Differential Treatment," *Boston College International and Comparative Law Review*, 27 (2004), 291, 293.
4. Robert E. Hudec, "GATT and the Developing Countries," *Colum. Bus. L. Rev.* (1992), 67.
5. Michael Hart and Bill Dymond, at 396.
6. Phil Levy, "Reciprocity And Trade Deals – Are Other Countries Taking Advantage?," *Forbes* (January 29, 2019); Simon Lester, "The 'Reciprocal Trade Act' Is Obviously Not About Free Trade But It's Also Not About Reciprocal Trade," Cato (January 25, 2019), at https://cato.org/blog/united-states-reciprocal-trade-act-neither-free-nor-reciprocal; Simon Lester and Inu Manak, "The Use and Abuse of 'Reciprocity' in Trade Policy," Cato (October 24, 2017), https://www.cato.org/blog/use-abuse-reciprocity-trade-policy.
7. GATT Article XVIII.
8. GATT Article XXXVIIIbis:3(b) and (c).
9. "Criteria for Identification of LDCs," United Nations Department of Economic and Social Affairs, Development Policy and Analysis Division, https://www.un.org/development/desa/dpad/least-developed-country-category/ldc-criteria.html.
10. "List of Least Developed Countries (as of December 2018)," United Nations Committee for Development Policy.
11. GATT Article XXXVI:8.
12. GATT Article XXXVI.
13. GATT Article XXXVII.
14. GATT Article XXXVIII.
15. GATT Article XXXVI:9.
16. Pallavi Kishore, "Special and Differential Treatment in the Multilateral Trading System," *Chinese Journal of International Law*, 13 (2014), 363, 373.
17. Waivers: Generalized System of Preferences, L/3545 (December 25, 1971), https://www.wto.org/gatt_docs/English/SULPDF/90840258.pdf.
18. The Enabling Clause.
19. Michael Hart and Bill Dymond, at 402–403.
20. Pallavi Kishore, at 375.

21. Marrakesh Agreement Establishing the World Trade Organization, https://www.wto.org/english/docs_e/legal_e/04-wto_e.htm.
22. WTO Committee on Trade and Development, "Special and Differential Treatment Provisions in WTO Agreements and Decisions," Note by the Secretariat, WT/COMTD/W219 (September 22, 2016).
23. Frank J. Garcia, at 296–297.
24. Doha Declaration, WT/MIN(01)/DEC/1 (November 20, 2001).
25. Doha Declaration, para. 2.
26. Implementation-Related Issues and Concerns, WTO Ministerial Conference, 4th Session, WT/MIN(01)/17, (decision of November 14, 2001).
27. Doha Declaration, para 37.
28. Doha Declaration, paras. 38–41.
29. Doha Declaration, paras. 42–43.
30. Doha Declaration, para. 44.
31. Rorden Wilkinson, Erin Hannah, and James Scott, "The WTO in Nairobi: The Demise of the Doha Development Agenda and the Future of the Multilateral Trading System," *Global Policy*, Vol. 7, No. 2 (April 21, 2016), 247–255.
32. *European Communities – Tariff Preferences*, WT/DS/AB/R (April 7, 2004).
33. WTO Dispute Settlement Understanding, Article 3.2.

5 Failure of the current approach to differential treatment

Trade scholars generally agree that the evolution of special and differential treatment in the WTO has largely been a history of failure. Having examined the evolution of such treatment in the multilateral trading system, Nicolas Lamp concluded that:

> Since its emergence in the 1960s, the principle of special and differential treatment in tariff negotiations has evolved in ways that have satisfied the aspirations of neither the developed nor the developing countries. The developed countries' hope that developing countries would 'graduate' to full reciprocity has largely remained unfulfilled. ... Developing countries' hope, on the other hand, that the principle could give rise to a 'right' to tariff reductions on non-reciprocal terms and to the formulation of 'specific rules' pursuant to which tariff reductions for the benefit of developing countries would be undertaken has also come to little.[1]

Not one country in the WTO-based trading system is fully satisfied with the economic benefits it has derived from being a part of the multilateral trading system, and all of the countries in the system feel in some way aggrieved.

In like vein, Patrick Low, Hamid Mamdouh, and Evan Rogerson – three former senior members of the WTO secretariat – have described the result of the decades of back and forth between developed and developing countries about special and differential treatment as a "minimalist bargain."[2] As they see it, "Developed countries offered unilateral tariff preferences on some products of export interest to developing countries instead of contract-bound most-favoured-nation (MFN) tariffs. In exchange, developing countries were 'obligation-lite' in terms of their own binding market access commitments, consistent with the principle of non-reciprocity."[3] The consequence of this trade-off?

> The "minimalist bargain" amounted to limited contractual market commitments from rich countries on products that mattered most to developing countries in exchange for limited or nonexistent market access commitments (tariff bindings) from many poorer countries. ... This more or less implicit arrangement paid scant attention to the core objective of fostering gains from trade through international cooperation. ... It created the equivalent of a trade class system and made it very difficult for countries with little or no accountability in the trading system to have a voice.[4]

Why has the current approach to special and differential treatment failed? It has failed because it is based on the premise that the growth of developing countries will be hastened if they postpone opening their markets to freer trade for as long as they can. The logic behind this premise is that, in affording more time and allowing more room for developing countries to erect and maintain trade barriers that insulate their domestic producers from foreign competition, SDT can help those countries climb more quickly up the ladder of development. This same logic also holds that infant industry protection can keep developing countries from being kicked off of the development ladder by developed countries that relied on trade protection to spark their own development.[5]

But this premise is mistaken. Protectionism may sometimes seem to work at first, but it never works for long. Protectionism does not work for infant industries or for other industries. It does not work for developed countries or for developing countries. Without the incentivising spur of competition that comes with freer trade, without the growth-creating innovations that freer trade brings and evokes, and without the domestic reforms that freer trade and a general openness to the wider world often inspire, the climb up the development ladder becomes steeper and longer. Protectionism is everywhere and always a prescription for slower economic growth, less economic dynamism, and fewer opportunities for everyone.

Michael Hart and Bill Dymond have explained the shortcomings of the current premise of SDT as follows:

> [P]roponents of special and differential treatment argue that developing countries, in the early stages of economic development, are not well placed to take full advantage of the opportunities created

by liberalization and the rules, and should thus be allowed to shelter their economies, at least initially, from the full application of the rules. Tempting as this argument may be, it is also misguided and perverse, more likely to retard than aid economic development. It is little more than a variant on the seductive, but much discredited, argument in favour of protecting infant industries, which continues to appeal to politicians and humanitarians, despite its failure both in practice and in gaining theoretical support. The benefits of an open economy, and the cost of a closed economy, are now among the most widely shared canons of economic orthodoxy, and yet discussion of special and differential treatment proceeds as if the issue remains an open question.[6]

As summed up by Arvind Panagariya, formerly chief economist for the Asia Development Bank and currently a professor at Columbia University, "Careful analysis shows that a logical case for import protection as the instrument to promote infant industries does not exist."[7] Invariably, the arguments made by advocates of infant industry protection emphasise instances where economic progress happened while a country pursued such a national policy. But, as Panagariya and many others have pointed out, the fact that one event occurs at the same time as another does not mean that the second event was caused by the first.[8] Correlation is not causation. A classic example is the United States, which imposed high tariffs on imported manufactured goods during the economic progress of the early days of the American republic. As Panagariya recalls, that such policies were in place while economic development was accelerating "does not clinch the case that those policies were responsible for the growth. Instead, the success may have resulted despite the inefficient policies because other domestic policies and institutions were favorable to rapid growth."[9]

In defending their own desire for trade protection for their infant industries, developing countries routinely cite what they perceive as the experience of the United States in growing economically because it had the shelter of high tariffs throughout the 19th century. (American protectionists often do the same in urging contemporary US protectionism.) But as economic historian Douglas Irwin explains:

> [T]he United States started out as a very wealthy country with a high literacy rate, widely distributed land ownership, stable government and competitive political institutions that largely guaranteed the security of private property, a large internal market with free trade in goods and free labor mobility across regions,

etc. Given these overwhelmingly favorable conditions, even very inefficient trade policies could not have prevented economic advances from taking place.[10]

Or, as this thought is expressed by Panagariya, "In other words, the United States grew not because of high tariffs but despite them."[11]

Government bureaucrats cannot know beforehand which infant industries they should endeavour to protect. They cannot pick which industries, which sectors, or which technologies would be the winners and losers in free commercial competition. Only the market can do that. Nor is protection likely to incentivise infant industries to invest in innovations. The first movers in those industries usually know that what they learn behind a wall of protectionism will soon spill over to domestic competitors that did not invest in learning at that time. These spillover effects cannot be controlled by protectionism.[12] So, the first movers in protected economies have less incentive to continue to innovate. Likewise, cutting local producers off from the competitive challenge of foreign competition does little to spur the industrialisation of rural economies, because "successful industrialization requires specialization in and exports of one set of industrial products and services while importing another set of industrial products and services."[13]

When a developing country (or, for that matter, any country) tries to shelter its economy from the competition that comes from being open to the wider world, it also shelters it from development. Some domestic producers may reap unearned profits from the economic privileges they obtain from amenable local governments. Some domestic workers in protected industries may savour the soothing illusion that their future has been assured. Some domestic politicians may pretend to their voters that, in insulating entrenched local interests from the challenges of competing in an economy open to the wider world, they are hurrying along the local process of development. But these politicians are not hastening development, they are impeding it. Special and differential treatment that excuses Members of the WTO from the full extent of their obligations, which are intended to help their economies reap the economic gains resulting from freer trade, is the very opposite of an approach that promotes their development.

The noble intent of those who seek special and differential treatment for developing countries in trade is "to support the marginalized and to make them less unequal."[14] Such treatment is envisaged as a form of affirmative action for narrowing the development divide.[15] Yet there is scant evidence that special and differential treatment serves this noble intent. Indeed, the limited empirical evidence that exists strongly suggests that this intent has been undermined by how SDT has been conceived and implemented over time. One of the few economic studies examining the effectiveness of SDT in promoting development is by Emanuel Ornelas. His 2016 study explains the unintended effects of the current approach to special and differential treatment in impeding development.

"The underlying justification for SDT," Ornelas reminds us, "is that temporary protection and preferential access to large markets could foster infant industries and help diversify the industrial base of developing countries, ultimately leading to sustained, faster economic growth."[16] He explains:

> It is assumed that greater access to the markets of industrialized economies will help them grow, but that they need more time and flexibility to liberalize their own markets. The key issues are therefore whether better access to the markets of developed countries can indeed help developing countries to grow (or to improve their economic performance more generally), and whether this can be achieved at the same time that they keep their own markets closed.[17]

Channeling Adam Smith, David Ricardo, and the legions of classical and neoclassical economists who have followed them, Ornelas dismisses the whole give-and-take of the purely political negotiating concepts of "concessions" and "reciprocity" by stating without reservation that, "The main theories of trade agreements offer no basis for SDT."[18] Like Panagariya and Irwin, he concludes that "the theoretical foundation for SDT is shaky and the empirical evidence inconclusive. Non-reciprocal preferences seem to foster exports of specific products and sector in beneficiary countries, but there is no support for SDT as a growth-promoting strategy. A widespread system of non-reciprocal preferences can also have the unintended consequence of slowing multilateral liberalization down."[19] Like most economists in the liberal tradition, Ornelas sees protectionism, by whatever name, as self-defeating and multilateral trade liberalisation as the proven path to growth and development.

Ornelas contends that "if anything, the design of SDT policies seems to be biased *against* the interests of developing countries."[20] The economic sectors in which many developing countries possess a comparative advantage in trade – especially agriculture and clothing – continue to face high tariffs in the developed world. GSP treatment for developing countries, while welcome, is discretionary and uncertain, and generally, it excludes those politically sensitive sectors in which those countries have the greatest comparative advantage. What is more, "intricate rules of origin also get in the way of the efficacy of preferences, creating sourcing distortions and bureaucratic hurdles that can render the preferences useless."[21]

Joost Pauwelyn points out, correctly, that the main losers from this biased arrangement are the least developed countries, which, as the poorest, stand to gain the most from further trade liberalisation and market access and are frustrated in their hopes for achieving development by the current structure of special and differential treatment.[22] In addition, there is an opportunity cost to accepting special and differential treatment. With respect to developing countries receiving such treatment, according to Ornelas, "[t]he problem is if a country does not liberalize itself, its import-competing sectors will remain a strong competitor for domestic resources, limiting the expansion of its exports."[23] Echoing his findings, the United Nations Development Programme sums up the failure of special and differential treatment as follows:

> Studies reveal that traditional SDT has not served developing countries well. Their trade interests, such as agriculture and apparel, have been liberalized slowly or not at all. It has also lessened the ability of the trade system to act as an external force for domestic reform. As a result, tariffs in developing countries are on average bound at the WTO at 30 percentage points above actual levels. Meanwhile, tariff liberalization among developing countries has been largely unilateral; it has not occurred from external negotiations.[24]

Special and differential treatment must be a means to achieve development and not an obstacle preventing it. Human, natural, and capital resources are everywhere and always limited. A decision to provide what the economists call "rents" – through sheltering trade protection to politically favoured domestic industries that face more efficient foreign competition – is also a decision to deny resources to other domestic industries that may have greater potential but lack comparable political favour. The division of labour that is trade is, fundamentally, about the allocation of limited resources. By allocating limited resources inefficiently, a resort to protectionism through the imposition of trade barriers impedes the pursuit of more productive opportunities that offer a better future. Thus, protectionism imposes what is often a considerable opportunity cost. Where protectionism prevails, the future is strangled by the past.

As President Trump complained, in many respects developing countries have often been "free riders" in the rules-based multilateral trading system. The United States and other developed countries have, time and again, made tariff cuts and other binding trade concessions and extended those concessions to all other WTO Members – including developing countries – under the multiplying operation of the basic WTO obligation of most-favoured-nation treatment. Under this principle, when tariffs and non-tariff trade barriers are lowered for one, they must be lowered for all. Meanwhile, developing countries have received the benefits of those generalised trade concessions made by developed countries, but often they have not been required to make comparable concessions of their own. Because developing countries have not been willing to make reciprocal concessions, it can be argued that they have not had the leverage in multilateral trade negotiations to secure the concessions they most seek from developed countries in sectors in which they can best compete, such as agriculture and clothing in exchange. In this way, "the expansion of their export sectors has been severely constrained by the lack of their own liberalisation."[25] As Hart and Dymond bluntly state: "By insisting they had rights but no obligations, developing countries surrendered their capacity to pursue those rights with any significant results."[26] They were, in effect, reduced to "second-class citizenship."[27]

Research by Kyle Bagwell and Robert Staiger on whether development goals can be achieved through multilateral trade negotiations concludes that "it is only by" developing countries "opening their markets that they will undergo the restructuring that is necessary to strengthen the competitiveness of their own industries."[28] (This could likewise be said, for example, of the US steel and aluminum industries.) The constraints on export expansion often caused by special and differential treatment deny developing country economies the benefits derived from the innovations and the learning spillovers that often accompany expanded exports, and that spread beyond export sectors throughout the entire economy.

In addition to the benefits derived by the private sector of a developing country from the more open economy resulting from full compliance with WTO obligations, there are also, more broadly, benefits to the public sector. In fact, and as the UNDP has observed, one of the principal benefits of WTO membership for developing countries is the impetus it can provide domestically for much-needed public reforms. This is especially the case where there is a reform-minded domestic government inclined towards more economic and political openness. The added international incentive of the external pressure to comply with WTO obligations can give governments the added political leverage they require to secure the domestic reforms it seeks.[29] This was the case, for instance, in China in the years immediately following its entry into the WTO. Most especially, in complying with the international rule of law, an example can be set for complying as well with the domestic rule of law. In endeavouring to open economies and governments to help create open societies, there is much to be said for the explanation and excuse that is often offered by many developing countries that are Members of the WTO: The WTO is making us do it.

Research by Man-Keung Tang and Shang-Jin Wei highlights the positive link between compliance with WTO obligations and successful domestic reforms.[30] Based on their study of the outcomes of the domestic reforms required by developing countries in complying with their accession agreements to membership in the WTO, they have concluded that the available evidence points towards a clear benefit for developing countries, not in moving *towards* more special and differential treatment, but rather in moving *away* from it. They argue that "a country can acquire a strong commitment to pro-growth policy reforms and convince investors that it has done so is by making the commitment a part of its international obligations," such as with an external commitment to reduce tariffs as a Member of the WTO.[31] They explain, "The value of such an external commitment is intuitive. While a government's unilateral announcement or implementation of a policy reform can be reversed or undone unilaterally, a policy reform embedded in an international treaty would involve a much higher cost of reversal."[32]

Tang and Wei's empirical results show that GATT/WTO accessions "are often associated with significant increases in growth and investment that last for about five years," noting that "the effects work only for those countries that have to undertake substantial reforms" and are not excused from undertaking such reform by their enjoyment of differential treatment.[33] And though this bump in the growth rate is temporary, "the economy is permanently larger (by 20%) as a result," and the benefits that result from these policy commitments "seem more pronounced among countries with poorer governance," which offers support for the theory "that binding policy changes enforced by a credible third party (WTO) serve as a (partial) substitute for good governance in promoting economic development."[34]

The continuing debate over the merits and the mechanisms of SDT is an echo of variations of a similar debate in the past: the debate over import substitution industrialisation policies shielding domestic producers in developing countries from import competition, advanced by Raul Prebisch and Hans Singer in the 1950s; the debate between Adam Smith and the mercantilists over the virtues of free trade versus protection in the 18th century; and, going all the way back to ancient Greece, the debate in classical Athens between those who advocated the self-sufficiency of autarky and those who favoured full engagement in the free flow of a bountiful Mediterranean trade. The debate in every era is always the same: are we, here where we live, better off if we are open or closed to receiving and engaging with the goods, services, capital, people, cultures, and ideas of the wider world? The debate is the ongoing debate between what Sir Karl Popper described in the title of his most famous book as *The Open Society and Its Enemies*.[35] Those in this debate who favour freer trade are on the side that seeks an open society where more people can make more individual decisions about how they choose to live. Thus, those on the side of freer trade are on the side of freedom.[36]

Endnotes

1. Nicolas Lamp, "How Some Countries Became 'Special': Developing Countries and the Construction of Difference in Multilateral Trade Lawmaking," *Journal of International Economic Law* 18 (2015): 743, 765–66.
2. Patrick Low, Hamid Mamdouh, and Evan Rogerson, "Balancing Rights and Obligations in the WTO – A Shared Responsibility," Government Offices of Sweden (2018), 5.
3. Ibid.
4. Ibid. at 10.
5. *See* Ha-Joon Chang, *Kicking Away the Ladder: Development Strategy in Historical Perspective* (London: Anthem World Economics, 2002).
6. Michael Hart and Bill Dymond, at 395.
7. Arvin Panagariya, *Free Trade and Prosperity: How Openness Helps Developing Countries Grow Richer and Combat Poverty* (New York: Oxford University Press, 2019), 55; on the shortcomings of the infant industry argument, see 55–60; *see also*, Arvind Panagariya, "Debunking Protectionist Myths: Free Trade, the Developing World, and Prosperity," Cato Economic Development Bulletin No. 31 (July 18, 2019).
8. Arvin Panagariya, *Free Trade and Prosperity*, at 52.
9. Ibid. at 51.
10. Douglas A. Irwin, "Review of *Kicking Away the Ladder: Development Strategy in Perspective*," at https://eh.net/book_reviews/kicking-away-the-ladder-development-strategy-in-historical-perspective.
11. Arvin Panagariya, *Free Trade and Prosperity*, at 51.
12. Ibid. at 50.
13. Ibid. at 47–48.

14. Pallavi Kishore, at 366.
15. Ibid.
16. Emanuel Ornelas, "Special and differential treatment for developing countries reconsidered," Center for Economic Policy Research (May 14, 2016), at https://voxeu.org/article/special-and-differential-treatment-developing-countries-reconsidered.
17. Emanuel Ornelas, *Special and Differential Treatment for Developing Countries*, in Kyle Bagwell and Robert W. Staiger, eds., 1B Handbook of Commercial Policy (Elsevier, 2016), at https://www.doi.org/10.1016/bs.hescop.2016.04.011.
18. Emanuel Ornelas, "Special and differential treatment for developing countries reconsidered."
19. Ibid.
20. Ibid.
21. Ibid.
22. Joost Pauwelyn, "The End of Differential Treatment for Developing Countries? Lessons from the Trade and Climate Change Regimes," *Review of European Community & International Environmental Law*, Vol. 22, No. 1 (2013): 29, 35.
23. Emanuel Ornelas, *Special and Differential Treatment for Developing Countries*.
24. UNDP, "World Development Report 2020," 218.
25. Emanuel Ornelas, "Special and differential treatment for developing countries reconsidered."
26. Michael Hart and Bill Dymond, at 415.
27. Ibid.
28. Robert D. Anderson, Comment on Kyle Bagwell and Robert D. Staiger, "Can the Doha Round Be a Development Round? Setting a Place at the Table," in Robert C. Feenstra and Alan M. Taylor, eds., *Globalization in an Age of Crisis: Multilateral Economic Cooperation in the Twenty-First Century* (Chicago, IL: University of Chicago Press, 2013), 91, 125.
29. See the following literature on compliance with international institutions and domestic politics: Goldstein, Judith, "International institutions and domestic politics: GATT, WTO, and the liberalization of international trade," *The WTO as an international organization* (1998): 138–151; Johns, Leslie, and B. Peter Rosendorff, "Dispute Settlement, Compliance and Domestic Politics," in *Trade disputes and the dispute settlement understanding of the WTO: An interdisciplinary assessment* (Emerald Group Publishing Limited, 2009); Moravcsik, Andrew, "The origins of human rights regimes: Democratic delegation in postwar Europe," *International Organization* (2000): 217–252; Landman, Todd, "The political science of human rights," *British Journal of Political Science* 35, no. 3 (2005): 549–572; Vreeland, James Raymond, "Political institutions and human rights: Why dictatorships enter into the United Nations Convention Against Torture," *International Organization* (2008): 65–101.
30. Man-Keung Tang and Shang-Jin Wei, "The Value of Making Commitments Externally: Evidence from WTO Accessions," National Bureau of Economic Research Working Paper No. 14582 (December 2008), at http://www.nber.org/papers/w14582.

31. Ibid at 2.
32. Ibid.
33. Ibid at 26.
34. Ibid at 26–27.
35. Karl R. Popper, *The Open Society and Its Enemies*, Volume 1, *The Spell of Plato,* and Volume 2, *The High Tide of Prophecy: Hegel, Marx, and the Aftermath*, 5th Edition, Revised (Princeton, NJ: Princeton University Press, 1971) [1945].
36. *See* James Bacchus, *Trade and Freedom* (London: Cameron May, 2004).

6 Complications created by China's emergence in the global economy

President Trump summarised the shared anxiety of many developed countries about special and differential treatment succinctly in his memorandum to the United States Trade Representative on July 26, 2019: "When the wealthiest countries claim developing-country status, they harm not only other developed economies but also economies that truly require special and differential treatment. Such disregard for adherence to WTO rules, including the likely disregard of any future rules, cannot continue to go unchecked."[1] The US proposal for reforming special and differential treatment stems from the concerns raised in this memorandum – concerns that predate the Trump presidency and have been raised by other US officials in the past, and will continue to be raised if the issue goes unresolved.

Although the United States has insisted that its calls for reform of SDT are not directed at any single country, it is nevertheless telling, as shown in Figure 6.1, that China is mentioned far more than any other country in the US proposal – 51 times (India is mentioned 23 times and Japan, South Korea and Singapore are both mentioned 15 times). This is entirely unsurprising, given that China's rapid economic rise since the turn of the century has altered trade terms and disrupted traditional trade expectations for the United States and other developed countries. It is the speed and the considerable impact of China's growth as a trading nation that have evoked calls from the Americans and from others for the Chinese to make additional trade concessions commensurate with their growing global economic status.

Whatever the broader intentions of the United States relating to the future of the multilateral trading system in offering its proposal, China is clearly the principal target of US frustration with the current approach to the provision of special and differential treatment. China fits within two of the four categories recommended by the United States for determining which Members of the WTO would be

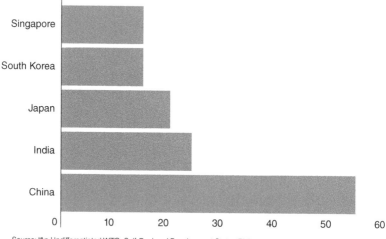

Source: "An Undifferentiated WTO: Self-Declared Development Status Risks Institutional Irrelevance, Communication from the United States," WT/GC/W/757/Rev.1, (February 14, 2019).

Figure 6.1 US proposal, top five country mentions.

ineligible for special and differential treatment. China is a member of the G20. China accounts for considerably more than 0.5 percent of world merchandise trade – 13 percent in 2019.[2] Indeed, in 2019, China ranked first in the world among exporters and importers in merchandise trade.[3] The United States ranked second.[4] In the view of the United States, this is ample reason why China should be treated as a developed country within the WTO and should not be afforded any special and differential treatment.

In response, China accuses the United States of cherry-picking certain statistics in making its case. This is a fair criticism, as the global debate over how best to measure poverty remains contested. In fact, in a report released in June 2019, the United Nations Conference on Trade and Development (UNCTAD) shows that China still has much work to do to eliminate poverty, and that, in discussing the issue of development, multiple economic, social, and environmental factors also play a role.[5] Since then, the worldwide outbreak of the Covid-19 pandemic, which began in China, has slowed the rate of continued poverty reduction in China.[6]

At the same time, the great economic transformations that have occurred in the developing world cannot be overlooked; nor can the very real differences among developing countries be denied. Although China concedes that there are differences among developing country members of the WTO, it maintains that what still unites all developing countries on the issue of SDT is the absence of "full and balanced development, [which] significantly outweigh[s] their differences."[7] China thus argues not only for the preservation of the status quo on self-declaration but also for strengthening SDT by fulfilling the call in Paragraph 44 of the Doha Ministerial Declaration in 2001 to review all differential treatment measures to ensure that they are "more precise, effective and operational."

The Chinese state that, in their view, as a legal matter, differential treatment is "an exception from the general trade rules."[8] On this legal point, though, China is mistaken. Special and differential treatment was not intended to be a general exception to the trade rules. Instead, eligibility for differential treatment has been limited and has been linked in specific ways to a variety of specific obligations that have been negotiated as part of the WTO agreements. The legal concept of special and differential treatment may be best understood as operating in three respects: as preferential access for developing country products in developed country markets (largely through GSP); as generally non-binding exhortations for technical assistance for lower-income economies provided by developed countries; and as discreet and distinctively qualified exemptions from certain specified WTO rules.[9] It is this varied assortment of specifically enunciated forms of special and differential treatment that is staunchly defended by China and by other developing countries.

As an avenue for development, however, this defence is misplaced; for, as an economist, Bernard Hoekman has observed, "the lure of nonreciprocal preferences has kept developing countries from exploiting the major source of gains from trade liberalization."[10] China, like other developing countries, has often not been able to make the most of trade liberalisation because it has shielded its most politically sensitive products and industries from import competition through tariff peaks and other restrictive measures, thus denying the Chinese economy as a whole of the multiple benefits that spur from foreign competition. In addition, China, like other developing countries, has often not been able to benefit fully from its comparative advantages because developed countries have been inclined to give the Chinese more market access only on products that matter less to Chinese trade.

It is, however, well worth examining some of China's points countering the US proposal in more detail, for they point towards what could become common ground on the metrics for assessing stages of development. The categories of indicators the United States advocates in its proposal are rational and defensible. However, the United States has offered only one set of various factors that can be used to differentiate between and among countries' levels of development. The crux of China's argument rests on the claim that there remains a stark development divide between the developed and developing world. This general point is irrefutable. But it poses two issues. The first is that China's comparison between developed and developing countries does nothing to counter the US SDT reform proposal, which is concerned with variations *among* developing countries. The second is the appropriateness of the variables chosen by China to determine the current extent of the development divide.

China uses gross domestic product (GDP) per capita to support its assertion that a development divide persists between developed and developing countries. In contrast, the United States uses gross national income (GNI) per capita to support its claim that this divide is narrowing and that different developing countries are at different stages of development. The main difference between these two metrics is that GNI is essentially GDP *plus* net receipts from abroad of compensation of employees, property income, and net taxes less subsidies on production. This means that the use of GNI adjusts for the income generated by residents regardless of where that income is generated. GDP only measures value added within a country. Given the global reach of the strongest economies, GNI tends to do a better job of capturing the state of a country's overall economic health. For this reason, GNI is used in the World Bank's calculation of country classifications for the purpose of issuing loans.

Reasoning likewise, the OECD has noted that GDP is not a good measure of a country's well-being because "GDP is primarily a gross measure of economic activities on the economic territory of a country, and the income generated through those activities," therefore, "[h]igh levels of GDP thus do not necessarily mean high levels of the (net) income flowing to the residents of an economy."[11] The use of GDP per capita may conceal vast disparities in individual incomes within a country. In a country with a population of one billionaire and one hundred paupers, the GDP per capita will be high, but one hundred people will be destitute. Those who favour Amartya Sen's capabilities approach to measuring development will point out that development is not a matter of counting the number of billionaires in a country. It is a matter of assessing overall human well-being.[12]

There was a marked growth in GDP per capita, especially for the poorest countries, between 1995 and 2017, as shown in Table 6.1. This growth, however, is better illuminated by using GNI per capita, as suggested by the United States. In terms of GNI, the interesting data point to note is the closing gap during those same years

Table 6.1 Gross domestic product (GDP) and gross national income (GNI) per capita, by Select Economic Groups, 1995–2017

Economy	GDP per capita, 1995	GDP per capita, 2017	GDP per capita, % change, 1995–2017	GNI per capita, 1995	GNI per capita, 2010	GNI per capita, 2017	GNI per capita, % change 1995–2017
Organisation for Economic Co-operation and Development members	29,029.40	39,295.09	35.4	28,648.44	36,368.37	40,037.25	39.8
Average economies in U.S. proposal	15,367.57	20,099.80	30.8	17,156.15	33,177.00	36,420.43	112.3
High income	31,309.26	42,784.88	36.7	31,304.25	40,239.73	44,364.56	41.7
Upper middle income	3,302.98	8,241.59	149.5	6,147.40	12,174.33	16,141.44	162.6
Middle income	2,185.45	5,021.18	129.8	4,507.00	8,405.93	11,015.90	144.4
Lower middle income	1,000.82	2,170.40	116.9	2,759.13	4,901.08	6,471.50	134.5
Low income	466.87	715.99	53.4	—	—	—	—
Least developed countries	492.13	936.21	90.2	1,314.50	2,073.75	2,598.64	97.7

Sources: "GDP per capita (constant 2010 US$)," World Bank Development Indicators; "GNI per capita, PPP (constant 2011 international$)," World Bank Development Indicators.

Notes: GDP per capita (1995) missing data for Qatar. GNI per capita missing data (all years): Low income; Antigua and Barbuda; Barbados; Saint Kitts and Nevis; Seychelles; Trinidad and Tobago; (1995): Bahrain; Indonesia; Kuwait; Macao; Oman; Qatar; Saudi Arabia; United Arab Emirates.

between OECD members and the 33 developing countries that would be captured in the US proposal. GNI per capita for OECD members was $28,648 in 1995 and $40,037 in 2017. For the 33 developing countries captured in the US proposal, GNI per capita was $17,156 in 1995 and grew by more than 110 percent to $36,420 in 2017. This is the equivalent of the average GNI per capita for an OECD member in 2010.

Although it is true that, in the other categories used by the World Bank for income classification, many countries trail behind the richest countries in per capita terms, the breadth of income discrepancies is not borne out in the data when looking at China and the other rapidly emerging economies that most concern the United States. For example, in 1995, South Korea had a GNI per capita (in 2011 international $) of $16,482. By 2017, this number for South Korea had grown to $35,944. By means of comparison, in 1995, the UK and France had a GNI per capita of $28,410 and $30,836, respectively; by 2017, these numbers had grown, respectively, to $39,216 and $39,935.[13] Thus, where the United Kingdom and France saw their GNI per capita grow by 38 percent and 30 percent, respectively, from 1995 to 2017, in contrast, Korea experienced a 118 percent increase in GNI per capita during those same years. It should therefore not be surprising that South Korea recently agreed to relinquish developing country status in future WTO negotiations.[14]

China's critique of the US proposal also points to high levels of poverty among many developing countries. While this is true on average, the reality is that 33 percent of the world's poor live in sub-Saharan Africa, and half of the world's poor are concentrated in just five countries – India, Nigeria, the Democratic Republic of Congo, Ethiopia, and Bangladesh ($1.90/a day).[15] India is the only one of these five countries that falls within one of the four categories set out in the US proposal for eliminating eligibility for special and differential treatment. By looking at the impoverished portions of the population of the three largest developing country markets – Brazil, China, and India – it becomes clear that there is significant differentiation among them. In 2011, the last complete year of data, the poverty headcount ratio (the percentage of the population living on less than $1.90 a day at 2011 international prices) was 4.7 percent in Brazil, 7.9 percent in China, and 21.2 percent in India. For Brazil, this figure slightly increased to 4.8 percent in 2017. For China, the poverty headcount dropped to 0.7 percent in 2015.[16] Although there is no recent data for India, it is notable that the poverty headcount there dropped from 38.2 percent in 2004, a 45 percent decrease in just 7 years.

The number of people living in extreme poverty has, of course, increased in all three of these countries during the coronavirus pandemic.[17] These numbers are all much higher now than they were when these numbers were calculated. Even so, the changes in these numbers during those years underscore that lumping all developing countries together in one category as "developing countries" is misleading. India's level of poverty, in particular, is higher than that of the two other countries. All this is a further illustration in support of the argument by the United States that there is a need to differentiate among the developing countries when considering their eligibility for SDT.

As Henry Gao and Weihuan Zhao, two leading Asian trade scholars have pointed out, "[i]n practical terms," the stakes for China in the debate over the fate of special and differential treatment in the WTO are "almost nothing."[18] These low stakes exist because China did not receive full developing country treatment when it became a Member of the WTO in 2001. Other developing countries had been required to cut their industrial tariffs from 42.7 percent to 31.4 percent in the Uruguay Round trade agreements that established the WTO; upon becoming a WTO Member, China agreed to cut its industrial tariffs to 9.5 percent. Similarly, other developing countries had agreed in the Uruguay Round trade agreements to cut their agricultural tariffs from 54 percent to 37.9 percent; in its WTO accession protocol, China agreed to cut its agricultural tariffs to 15.1 percent. Moreover, China agreed to an 8.5 percent *de minimis* level for its agricultural support, which is below the 10 percent *de minimis* level allowed for other developing countries in the WTO Agreement on Agriculture. In addition, where other developing countries are permitted under the WTO rules to impose export taxes, China agreed when it joined the WTO not to impose export prices on numerous products.[19] Gao and Zhao conclude:

> China has received hardly any of the benefits that accrue to developing countries when it became a WTO member, other than the ability to use the title 'developing country.'...[I]t enjoys little preferential treatment for itself, partly because it has eschewed special benefits, partly because most of the transition benefits that were available to it have expired, partly because some of the provisions available to it are essentially voluntary on the part of the country offering them, and partly because many of the benefits available to developing countries are not available to developing countries with large export shares."[20]

Given all this, it can be argued that the trade grievances of the United States and other developed countries against China should not be attributed to China's status in the WTO as a developing country or to its enjoyment of special and differential treatment under WTO rules. Whatever the merit of these trade grievances, there is a cause to conclude that their source must be located elsewhere.

Gao points out that, in recent trade negotiations, China has received less special and differential treatment than other developing countries. This underscores a broader claim made by China and the nine other developing countries in countering the US proposal that "though the self-declared developing Members have the right to utilise differential treatment, they always make their contribution as much as they can."[21] To justify this claim, the ten countries point to the Trade Facilitation Agreement (TFA) as an example of how the grant of special and differential treatment does not imperil multilateral trade negotiations. This point deserves emphasis. The TFA is a departure from past WTO agreements in that its signatories have specifically identified short- and long-term implementation timelines and have also noted those provisions where technical assistance will be required for implementation. This TFA approach is novel in that it links special and differential treatment to an identified need, as opposed to a general opt-out on certain commitments. In this respect, it could help point towards an alternative approach to differential treatment.

Given the ongoing trade confrontation between the two countries, it might be assumed, at first glance, that the US proposal is targeting exclusively at China. Two-way trade tensions between the United States and China tend to overshadow other trade concerns. But, despite its tacit targeting of China, as evidenced by the extent to which it dwells on China in its reform proposal, the United States appears to be attempting a broader rebalancing of the multilateral trading system. China is, in the eyes of the United States, simply one of the clearest examples of why the current regime is unbalanced. All the same, given recent events, the Chinese can be forgiven for thinking that the US proposal is addressed mainly to their growing presence in the international trading system.

All in all, since China joined the WTO in 2001, the rules of the multilateral trading system have been effective tools for gradually integrating China into the rules-based world trading system. Like other developing countries, China has employed WTO obligations as leverage to help make market-oriented domestic reforms, and China has complied with rulings against it in WTO dispute settlement at about the same rate as other major economies.[22] There are, undeniably, real and valid concerns about some of China's behaviour in the international economy and valid questions about the extent to which WTO rules may need to be modernised to be able to address some of the issues posed by China's participation in the multilateral trading system. These concerns have intensified in recent years as the Chinese government has seemed to turn away from market reforms and back towards a more state-directed economy. The challenge is how to deal with these concerns in a constructive way that leads to a mutually acceptable solution. Finding and forging a consensus on an alternative approach to differential treatment can be part of that solution.

Many are rightly sceptical that China, the United States, and other WTO Members can ever reach an agreement on a definition of a developing country as a means of identifying which countries should be eligible for SDT. The United States and other developed countries may propose all the statistical categories they wish for identifying legal lines that demarcate the difference between developed and developing status, but achieving consensus on this issue is likely to be impossible. Furthermore, such an effort is unlikely to yield comprehensive SDT reform. That said, developing countries may ultimately be willing to support a proposal that distinguishes countries based on their stages of development. To date, no developing country has indicated any genuine support for such a proposal. It is, however, possible that the voices of larger emerging economies such as China and India are obscuring those of other developing countries that may see the virtue in making such finer distinctions, since, increasingly, many developing countries are struggling to compete not only with the goods and services of the United States and other developed countries but also with growing competition from China, India, and other newly emerging economies.

Endnotes

1. Presidential Memorandum for the United States Trade Representative, "Memorandum on Reforming Developing-Country Status in the World Trade Organization."
2. World Trade Organization, "World Trade Statistical Review 2020" (Geneva: WTO, 2020), 82.
3. Ibid.
4. Ibid.
5. Richard Kozul-Wright, et al., "From Development to Differentiation: Just how much has the world changed?" UNCTAD Research paper No. 33 (June 2019), at https://unctad.org/en/PublicationsLibrary/ser-rp-2019d5_en.pdf.
6. World Bank, "China Economic Update – July 2020," at https://worldbank.org/en/country/china/publication/china-economic-update-july-2020.

7. WTO General Council, Minutes of the Meeting, WT/GC/M/176 (February 28, 2019) para. 7.8.
8. Ibid., para. 7.10.
9. These dimensions are explained in detail in Bernard Hoekman, Constantine Michalopoulos, and L. Alan Winters, "More Favorable and Differential Treatment of Developing Countries," World Bank, Development Research Group, Working Paper 3107 (Washington, D.C.: World Bank Group, August 2003).
10. Bernard Hoekman, "More Favorable Treatment of Developing Countries: Ways Forward," in *Trade, Doha, and Development: A Window into the Issues*, ed. Richard Newfarmer (Washington DC: World Bank Group, 2006), 214.
11. "Irish GDP up by 26.3% in 2015?" OECD (October 2016), at http://www.oecd.org/sdd/na/Irish-GDP-up-in-2015-OECD.pdf.
12. Our thanks to the multi-talented Professor Joseph Janeti of UCLA for this observation.
13. World Bank Development Indicators, GNI per capita, PPP (constant 2011 international $).
14. Hannah Monicken, "Korea poised to forgo WTO developing status, meeting a key U.S. demand," *Inside U.S. Trade* (September 5, 2019), at https://insidetrade.com/daily-news/korea-poised-forgo-wto-developing-status-meeting-key-us-demand; Jane Chung and Joori Roh, "South Korea to give up developing country status in WTO talks," *Reuters* (October 24, 2019).
15. World Bank, "Poverty Outlook," at https://www.worldbank.org/en/topic/poverty#a.
16. World Bank Development Indicators, "Poverty headcount ratio at $1.90 a day (2011 PPP) (% of population)."
17. Daniel Gerszon Mahler, Christopher Lakner, R. Andres Castaneda Aguilar, and Haoyu Wu, "Updated estimates of the impact of COVID-19 on global poverty," World Bank Blogs (June 8, 2020), at https://blogs.worldbank.org/opendata/updated-estimates-impact-covid-19-global-poverty.
18. Henry Gao and Weihuan Zhao, "Myth busted: China's status as a developing country gives it few benefits in the World Trade Organization," *The Conversation* (October 6, 2019).
19. Ibid.
20. Henry Gao and Weihuan Zhao, "Myth busted: China's status as a developing country gives it few benefits in the World Trade Organization."
21. WT/GC/W/765/Rev.2, para. 5.15.
22. James Bacchus, Simon Lester and Huan Zhu, "Disciplining China's Trade Practices at the WTO," Cato Institute Policy Analysis No. 856 (November 15, 2018), at https://object.cato.org/sites/cato.org/files/pubs/pdf/pa856.pdf.

7 An alternative approach to differential treatment

Promoting trade promotes development, and restricting trade restricts development. The rhetoric of the usual defence of special and differential treatment evades this basic fact. Perhaps, most notable in that rhetoric is what is missing from it. When defending SDT, developing countries speak volumes in what they do *not* say. They do not cite any concrete examples of how their development has been advanced by special and differential treatment, particularly in the way that it is currently structured in the WTO agreements. Could this be because there are no examples? To be able to identify examples of how special and differential treatment can advance development, and not impede it, we must have a broader understanding of the meaning of development, and we must design an alternative approach to SDT that proceeds from that understanding towards the pursuit of trade in a way that enables a full flourishing of humanity.

Unquestionably, the full development of all the 164 Members of the multilateral trading system is a goal of the multilateral trading system. At the outset, in the preamble to the Marrakesh Agreement of 1994 establishing the World Trade Organization, Members of the new WTO agreed on the "need for positive efforts designed to ensure that developing countries, and especially the least developed among them, secure a share in the growth of international trade commensurate with the needs of their economic development."[1] This commitment was reaffirmed in the final declaration of the WTO Ministerial Conference in Nairobi in 2015, which stated, "The majority of WTO Members are developing country Members. We seek to place their needs and interests at the centre of the work of the WTO. We reaffirm the centrality of development in the WTO's work ...."[2] Alas, this resolute reaffirmation of the centrality of development to the multilateral trading system occurred at the same time as the demise of the Doha Development Round.

Often overlooked in WTO negotiations and other deliberations, but nestled in the preamble to the Marrakesh Agreement, is a shared commitment by the Members of the WTO to conduct their "trade and economic endeavor ... with a view to ... allowing for the optimal use of the world's resources in accordance with the objective of sustainable development, seeking both to protect and preserve the environment and to enhance the means for doing so in a manner consistent with their respective needs and concerns at different levels of economic development."[3] Because all the Members of the WTO are also members of the United Nations, presumably what they envisage as "sustainable development" in the Marrakesh Agreement is consistent with what they agreed to in the UN Sustainable Development Goals of 2015.[4] The members of the United Nations have defined sustainable development by describing the details of what it should look like in the SDGs. As set out in the 17 global goals and the 169 targets of the United Nations Agenda for 2030, sustainable development is consistent with how it was first articulated in the landmark report of the United Nations Commission on Environment and Development in 1987; it is "development that meets the needs of the present without compromising the ability of future generations to meet their own needs."[5]

This view of sustainable development must begin with the primacy of human freedom. Through the prism of his own perspective of "development as freedom," Amartya Sen tells us that "[d]evelopment is fundamentally an empowering process" that must always be about individual human beings.[6] From this premise, he reasons that:

> If the importance of human lives lies not merely in our living standard and need-fulfillment, but also in the freedom we enjoy, then the idea of sustainable development has to be correspondingly reformulated. There is cogency in thinking not just about sustaining the fulfillment of our needs, but more broadly about sustaining – or extending – our freedom (including the freedom to meet our needs). Thus recharacterized, sustainable freedom can be broadened ... to encompass the preservation, and when possible expansion, of the substantive freedoms and capabilities of people today 'without compromising the ability of future generations' to have similar – or more – freedom.[7]

The preamble to the Marrakesh Agreement suggests this more comprehensive view of development as sustainable development, and of sustainable development as an empowering process for attaining sustainable freedom for people as individuals in every part of the world.

This broader view of development is embedded in the preamble of the Marrakesh Agreement, and it should be the lodestar of the Members of the WTO in seeking economic advancement. In their search for freedom through sustainable development, this broader view of development should guide them, too, in shaping and providing the content of any special and differential treatment for developing countries in the WTO. This broader view of development includes the various traditional measures of economic advance, but it also encompasses other dimensions of development, as outlined in the SDGs, such as ending poverty and hunger, promoting quality education, providing employment, securing public health, fostering innovation, achieving gender equity, and fighting climate change, which all further the full flourishing of human freedom.

In this more expansive view of what development means, sustainable freedom will not be attained by the billions of individual people who live in developing countries unless and until their eyes and their lives are opened to the instructive challenges and to the boundless opportunities of the wider world – including those created by international trade. Engaging in trade is not merely a matter of commerce. It is a means for achieving the end of human freedom and for promoting the broadest fulfillment of both individual and national potential.[8]

The alternative approach that is needed to special and differential treatment in the WTO must be framed through the lens of this broader view of what development means. It is in part for this reason that the right alternative approach to determining precisely how much and what kind of SDT may be needed to help people in developing countries must consider, as development economist William Easterly has put it, "The cause of poverty is the absence of political and economic rights, the absence of a free political and economic system that would find the technical solutions to the poor's problems."[9] And it is in part for this reason also that the right alternative approach to according special and differential treatment must take into account the varied aspects and stages of development towards such a political and economic system. The Members of the WTO must no longer be divided into two opposing camps along the single line of a stunted view of the meaning of development. The countries that comprise the multilateral trading system must no longer be labelled solely in either/or terms as "developed" or "developing" countries. Such a dichotomous classification of countries is insufficient in categorising the varieties and complexities of development in the global economy of the 21st century.

Today's world economy is vastly more complicated than that. There is a need for considerably more nuance instead of the simplistic rhetoric we are increasingly offered. In trade, there is a need now, more than ever, for making finer distinctions, case by case, product by product, and sector by sector. With the multilateral trading system increasingly threatened on numerous fronts, with the system's most steadfast supporters worried that it may soon be sidelined into irrelevance, and with the historical divide between developed and developing countries wider than ever before in the councils of the WTO, there is an urgent need for an alternative approach to SDT that is reflective of the reality of the current economic shape of the world and is flexible in the frameworks it uses to further development.

What does an alternative approach to special and differential treatment look like?

As a starting point, the focus of special and differential treatment in the WTO should not be on more exclusion. It should be on more inclusion. As Low, Mamdouh, and Rogerson put it, succinctly, special and differential treatment in trade "should enable rather than exempt."[10] The basic flaw in the current approach to differential treatment in the WTO is that it revolves around seeking exemptions from WTO obligations instead of on helping developing countries comply with the rules and thus integrate fully into the multilateral trading system. This current approach limits the ability of individuals in developing countries to attain sustainable freedom by preventing them from having access to much of what they need from the wider world to enable their personal development. Those harmed by special and differential treatment are not the people living in developed countries; instead, they are the people living in developing countries.

Hart and Dymond agree with this criticism as a matter of international political economy. In their own critique of the current WTO approach to SDT, they maintain that "[d]eveloping countries can only 'secure a share in the growth of world trade commensurate with the needs of their economic development,'" as contemplated in the preamble to the Marrakesh Agreement, "by taking full advantage of the trade regime. By contrast, further weakening the regime to accommodate additional ill-conceived special and differential measures will not help developing countries but will harm the trade regime, including the trade interests of developing countries and especially the least-developed of them."[11] One significant potential harm is that providing developing countries with too many exemptions from WTO trade obligations for too many wrong reasons will undermine the basic principle of non-discrimination that is the very foundation of the multilateral trading system while accomplishing little or nothing towards achieving the freedom of sustainable development for the people who live in those countries.

In expressing the need for SDT to focus on enablement instead of exemption, Hart and Dymond pointedly observe that, despite the "less-than-stellar record" of such treatment, "much of the public discourse regarding special and differential treatment assumes there is a strong case establishing its efficacy."[12] As they see it:

> If there is any justification for special and differential treatment in the WTO, it revolves around the capacity of developing countries to implement their WTO commitments and the priority they should assign to gaining such capacity .... The economic issue is ... whether poorer countries are pursuing appropriate policies to promote economic development and alleviate poverty, and whether developed countries are prepared to adopt programmes and policies that support these efforts.[13]

The right approach to special and differential treatment will not try to isolate and insulate individual people in developing countries from foreign trade or other aspects of the wider world but will empower them with sustainable freedom so they can flourish at home and abroad.

With the imperative of fashioning an alternative approach to development through the right kind of special and differential treatment in mind, two separate but related questions arise for the Members of the WTO. The first is which countries should be eligible for special and differential treatment? The second is what specific special and differential treatment should these countries receive? If these two questions are answered appropriately in WTO negotiations, then the world trading system will have much more hope for dealing with the development dimension to international trade, and for attaining the global goals for sustainable development by the UN target date of 2030.

On the first of these two questions, many are rightly sceptical that the Members of the WTO can ever achieve a consensus on an agreed definition of a developing country as a means of identifying which countries should be eligible for differential treatment, as noted earlier. The United States and other developed countries may propose all the statistical categories they wish for identifying legal lines that demarcate the different stages of development. But, for example, Low, Mamdouh, and Rogerson, with a combined experience in the trading system covering many decades, conclude, realistically, that "Modifying its own status quo is not something the WTO could easily do. The likelihood of reaching agreement on a formal categorisation of developing countries at the WTO is on a very narrow spectrum of somewhere between exceedingly remote and impossible."[14]

These three veterans of the trading system then go on to add, however, that "many developing WTO members would likely support finer distinctions among their number."[15] To be sure, to date, not one developing country seems to have indicated any support for any such "finer distinctions." Given the vast economic differences between and among the more than 100 developing countries that are Members of the WTO, perhaps, differing views would emerge in the course of any formal negotiations that may be launched by the WTO on the future of special and differential treatment. And perhaps, in the right negotiating circumstances, some developing countries would be more willing to engage on the highly emotional issue of SDT than seems now to be the case.

In such an event, it may become easier to reach a consensus in support of using certain agreed statistical categories to help identify which countries are eligible for differential treatment – more so if this is attempted within a negotiating context in which developing countries are offered some of the concessions they have long sought from developed countries on such matters as agricultural subsidies, trade remedies, and textiles and clothing. Yet, saying that reaching a consensus on eligibility requirements for special and differential treatment would be easier in such circumstances is not the same as saying that it would be easy. It would not. Complexities in reaching an agreement on appropriate categories would surely abound and domestic political consideration would complicate matters further in international negotiations.

To name only one WTO Member, the United States has made a concrete proposal for identifying which countries are eligible for differential treatment. As Anabel González has pointed out, "the US proposal is flawed. It would disallow India, Indonesia, and Vietnam, for example, to self-declare, even though they are certainly developing countries."[16] Yet, González would no doubt readily acknowledge that in contrast to so many of its other actions relating to the WTO since the inauguration of President Trump in January 2017, the United States has, at least on this divisive issue, not just complained without suggesting a solution but has in fact made a specific recommendation for reform. Most constructively, the submission of the US proposal has prompted a lively debate on the issue of special and differential treatment in the WTO that is long overdue.

This gathering WTO debate seems ripe for truly substantive engagement on this central issue in the multilateral trading system. It should be continued in full-blown multilateral negotiations. And only once the first question of which countries should be eligible for special and differential treatment is answered, can we begin to narrow in on the answer to the second, that is, what specific special and differential treatment should these countries receive? As we and numerous others have noted in detail above, a focus solely on the exemption from future obligations will not suffice. In fact, given the variation in levels of development among developing countries, it would make more sense to tailor special and differential treatment to their specific needs. This requires, to begin, a broader view of development premised on the understanding that development is rooted in individual human flourishing.

To encourage this view of development in the way that special and differential treatment is approached, we make two suggestions for these negotiations that can help avoid a divisive debate over *what a developing country is*, broadly speaking. First, a country's self-declared status should have no specific or automatic effect in the context of trade negotiations. WTO Members must no longer be divided into opposing camps along the single line of an antiquated and stunted view of the meaning of development. Except for LDCs, the countries that comprise the WTO-based multilateral trading system must no longer be labelled solely as either "developed" or "developing" countries. Second, SDT should be awarded on a case-by-case, product-by-product, and sector-by-sector basis. There would thus be no need for the WTO to adopt any all-purpose definition of the content of SDT. Rather, SDT should be defined as each alleged need for it arises in trade negotiations.

This new, case-by-case approach to SDT should centre on the development of human capabilities. It should not focus on excusing developing countries from WTO obligations but rather on the concrete actions that developing countries must take to enable their citizens to achieve better economic outcomes as a part of a full human flourishing. The proposal made by China and nine other developing countries acknowledges Amartya Sen's broader approach to development but does not explain how this approach could inform new thinking on SDT. As we have previously explained, Sen's approach is predicated on his conviction that "development can be seen...as a process of expanding the real freedoms that people enjoy" to make individual choices.[17] Therefore, the goal of development should be to expand the individual's freedom of choices, that is, to expand "the 'capabilities' of persons to lead the kind of lives they value – and have reason to value."[18] As evidenced by its wide use by the United Nations, as well as by the submission of China and the other nine countries to the WTO, this conviction is widely shared among developed and developing countries alike. It could be integrated into new criteria for evaluating requests for SDT.

Towards the end of establishing metrics for a new approach towards awarding SDT, helpfully, the United States has proposed four criteria that could be employed as part of determining eligibility for differential treatment in specific instances – membership in the OECD, membership in the G20, classification as a "high income" country by the World Bank, and accounting for 0.5 percent or more of global merchandise trade (imports and exports). These four criteria should be among the ingredients mixed in making a solution but should not be used to lump countries into broad categories of "developed" or "developing" because these are inadequate in presenting a complete picture of human development. As China, India, South Africa, Indonesia, and other developing countries that have spoken up in opposition to the US proposal have contended, reliance on these four categories alone would be too limiting. They rightly say that the four categories identified by the United States are indicative of some aspects of development but not of all. What is more, these four categories favoured by the United States do not reflect the broader concept of development as sustainable freedom for sustainable development.

In furtherance of this broader view of development, and as China and other developing countries have contended in their counters to the US proposal, added to the four categories identified by the United States in any consideration of eligibility for differential treatment should be additional indicators that better reveal the continued persistence and pervasiveness of poverty in even the most rapidly emerging developing economies. Indicators that measure overall human well-being should be included in this. In particular, the four categories proposed by the United States should be supplemented by the United Nations' Human Development Index, which, like the United Nations' annual Human Development Report, is a broader measurement specially constructed to quantify Sen's capabilities approach to development as freedom.

The Human Development Index (HDI) is a statistical tool employed by the United Nations to measure a country's overall level of development in its social as well as its economic dimensions. In addition to general economic conditions, the HDI captures other dimensions of development that reflect the quality of life and living standards. The HDI is a broader numerical way of gauging development that is based on measuring the health of a people, their level of educational attainment, and their standard of living. Generally speaking, in calculating the HDI, health is measured by life expectancy at birth, education is measured by the expected years of schooling for children of school-entering age and the mean of years of schooling for adults aged 25 years or more, and standard of living is measured by per capita gross national income.[19] In the rankings of 189 countries in the 2018 HDI, Mexico ranked 74th, Brazil 79th, China 86th, Vietnam 116th, and India 130th. Norway ranked 1st, Switzerland 2nd, Australia 3rd, Germany 5th, Japan 9th, and the United States 13th.[20]

In addition to the HDI, other measures the WTO should use in determining, on a case-by-case basis, a country's eligibility for SDT include the global indicators the United Nations has developed for calculating a country's progress towards the fulfillment of the SDGs. These indicators measure progress towards accomplishing the full range of all 17 SDGs. All WTO Members have agreed on these indicators as well as on the targets and goals of the SDGs. Use of these indicators would contribute much to making trade an affirmative agent for accomplishment of the SDGs. It would also be in keeping with the promise in the preamble to the Marrakesh Agreement that trade will be pursued consistently with the objectives of sustainable development. Where countries are struggling to achieve results, a case can be made for enhanced capacity building, for instance.

Compromise will be necessary to adopting a new approach to SDT. And compromise will require agreement by WTO Members on clear metrics for determining a country's development needs in different negotiating areas. González recommends that eligibility for special and differential treatment should depend, first, on a country's share of world trade in a particular sector, and, second, on whether that share is large enough to affect world prices in that sector.[21] In her view, a country might be "developed" in one sector of trade while still "developing" in another. Nowhere does development in all trade sectors occur on the same timeline. Every country, developed and developing alike, is always more competitive globally in some sectors of trade than in others. To implement her creative suggestion, different specific solutions would need to be agreed by WTO members on different products and in different sectors of trade, including the agreed metrics for assessment. We support this approach, which reflects the reality of the new shape of the global economy. For instance, in negotiations over fisheries subsidies, those countries that subsidise the most should take on the strongest commitments to reduce their subsidies.

Equally creative is a suggestion by Joel Trachtman, who states, "Perhaps it is time to substitute a more refined, and at the same time more flexible, mechanism, one which allows an exception from WTO commitments for any measure by any state where the measure is found to have reasonably anticipated poverty reduction effects, so long as the trade burdens on foreign powers are not disproportionate in relation to the poverty reduction benefits."[22] To implement Trachtman's novel suggestion, WTO Members would need to agree on a reliable means of evaluating a prospective measure's expected effects in reducing poverty. If not immediately available, such metrics might be devised by the WTO Secretariat together with other relevant international institutions and then adopted by the Members of the WTO. In addition, there would be a need for agreement on how best to determine beforehand whether the trade burdens of the proposed SDT measure on other countries would be disproportionate to its anticipated benefits in reducing poverty.

High-level negotiations are necessary to move this discussion forward and provide a clear basis for evaluating SDT. In these negotiations, all WTO Members will need to agree on the appropriate metrics for gauging development needs and how those needs translate into varying levels of obligations. There may be a path forward to a negotiated compromise within the proposals made thus far. Such a compromise could be adopted as a set of nonbinding but illustrative general guidelines by which requests for SDT could be assessed, agreed upon by all WTO Members in the form of a ministerial declaration. Undergirding such a declaration should be a restatement of the important link between trade and sustainable development. These guidelines could then serve as a resource for guiding future negotiations on SDT without becoming obstacles to appreciating the degree of nuance necessary to find common ground for consensus on any specific SDT request.

Ultimately, WTO Members will have to decide the circumstances under which countries will be eligible for SDT. This decision can best be made on a case-by-case basis. A case-by-case approach would eliminate much of the consternation over self-declaration. If decisions were made case by case, then the value of declaring oneself a "developing country" would be reduced; for, whatever a country's claimed status, the eligibility for and the content of SDT would be determined during negotiations by the facts and the circumstances of each case. Importantly, this would lead to a more data-driven approach to the grant of special and differential treatment.

Relying on "self-declaration" as a guide for providing SDT is fraught with peril during the course of trade negotiations. Consider, for instance, the puzzling ambiguities of the US proposal on this matter.

The United States has been less than clear about whether it wants the WTO to continue to practise self-declaration. If a WTO member has previously self-declared that it is a developing country, and if it falls within one of the four categories proposed as criteria by the United States, will that country thus have to relinquish its developing country status under the US proposal? Also, if a country does not self-declare that it is a developing country but falls outside the parameters of the four categories identified by the United States, will it be treated as a developing country even though it has not declared that it is one? The US Ambassador to the WTO under President Trump, Dennis Shea, told the WTO General Council, "I want to be clear that the US proposal does not require any Member to change its declaration of its development status."[23] Yet, in its 2019 proposal, the United States seemed to imply that precisely the opposite is the case – that only LDCs and other countries that do not fall within any of its four preferred categories should be treated as developing countries. Questions such as these underscore the difficulty of ever reaching a consensus in the WTO on general eligibility requirements for special and differential treatment, and why an alternative approach to the issue is therefore needed that moves away from these two broad categorical distinctions.

In addition, throughout the seven decades of the rules-based trading system, there has never been a single all-encompassing rule identifying the content of SDT. Special and differential treatment has instead been identified anew on each occasion when it has been sought, based on the context of each discrete trade agreement and the specific obligations it entails. The most practical solution for the ever-practical negotiators of WTO trade agreements would be to continue this long-standing practice of determining the content of special and differential treatment case by case. There is no need in the WTO for a general definition of the content of special and differential treatment. Thus, there is also no need for what would most likely be futile negotiations trying to reach consensus on a definition.

A novelty in the approach we propose is its focus on individual countries. In the past, the case-by-case approach to SDT has largely made all self-declared developing countries eligible for the same carefully negotiated type of SDT. Our case-by-case approach would focus on each developing country individually and would make distinctions on that country's eligibility for, and the content of their SDT based on the facts and circumstances relevant to that country. As in the past, certain categories of special and differential treatment with respect to certain WTO obligations might be predetermined in WTO negotiations. But, in the future, each country would have to convince other countries during negotiations that it should receive a specific form of SDT for a specific time, product, or sector. Essentially, any country that requested a specific instance of SDT would have to make its case and provide evidence to support it.

The general provision of special and differential treatment to least developed countries (LDCs) should continue. LDC status is already determined by economic criteria, including a clear metric for graduation. Furthermore, given the heavier negotiating burden imposed by our new approach, LDCs, unlike many other developing countries, would not have the immediate capacity to negotiate their need for SDT on a case-by-case basis. And yet, the WTO trading system should place much more emphasis on helping LDCs escape their current need for SDT with measures such as technical assistance and capacity building. In this respect, as has been suggested, the TFA offers a good starting point. The goal for LDCs must not be consignment to a permanent underclass of non-developed states. Rather, the goal must be eventual graduation from their current LDC status, and working towards being fully integrated into the WTO and expected to meet all commensurate obligations of WTO membership as soon as possible. When they graduate from LDC status, they could begin to negotiate each of their requests for SDT on a case-by-case basis, just like other developing countries. The United Nations reports that the LDCs "have progressed too slowly" towards achievement of the Sustainable Development Goals "largely due to scant progress in structural transformation."[24] The structural transformation so much needed in these poorest countries in the world cannot be accomplished without more openness to trade and without their fuller integration into the multilateral trading system.

With this new approach, even if self-declaration continues, developing countries would not automatically receive all forms of SDT. They could conceivably receive one form of SDT for certain obligations in negotiations but not others. The burden would be on the country requesting SDT to provide evidence that it is needed in that specific instance. For example, under this new approach, when WTO Members claim developing country status in relation to a particular traded product or trade sector, their eligibility for SDT would be determined, in part, by the impact of their production, sale, and export of that product or in that trade sector on the worldwide market prices and distribution of shares in that product or sector. Under this alternative, case-by-case approach, if a request was made for special and differential treatment for product A or sector A, it would be of no significance whether the country seeking SDT was competitive in product B or sector B. The negotiations would focus entirely on A.

This alternative approach to special and differential treatment would eliminate much of the consternation over self-declaration, as evidenced by the United States in making and describing its proposal. With the new version of the case-by-case approach, it would not be necessary for any country that has already self-declared its status as a developing country to renounce that status. Self-declared status would have no specified or automatic effect in the case-by-case negotiations on individual products and sectors. So, there would be little point to self-declaration in the future. The value of having declared developing country status, such as it is, would be much reduced by embracing the revised case-by-case approach; whatever a country's claimed status, the eligibility for and the content of special and differential treatment would be determined during negotiations by the facts and the circumstances of each case.

Similarly, the importance of the concept of graduation from special and differential treatment would be much diminished. It would still have the same significance for the least developed countries, but, for all other developing countries, there would be no such clear line of demarcation. There would be no single point of graduation to overall developed country status. In any event, the goal of LDCs would not be merely graduation from differential treatment but would be the fulfillment of all the obligations in the WTO agreements as a means of securing sustainable freedom for their people.

This new case-by-case approach to providing special and differential treatment would also allow ample space for the nuances that characterise the economy of the 21st century. In this global economy, Brazil can have a pivotal impact on the global soybean market while millions of Brazilians are still mired in poverty in favelas. The spires of skyscrapers can shine in the Shanghai sun while millions of Chinese remain immiserated in the countryside. When using this new approach to making determinations about differential treatment on a case-by-case basis, soybeans shipped by Brazil and some services provided from Shanghai may well not warrant special and differential treatment. At the same time, for other traded products and for other trade sectors, SDT may well be justified for Brazilian and Chinese goods and services in helping advance the continued development of their people. Nuances such as these should figure into making determinations about both eligibility for SDT and the content of it. In consideration of these nuances, distinctions will necessarily have to be made between and among different developing countries in different products and sectors of trade. Thus, whenever special and differential treatment is requested by a country for trade in a product or in a sector, the central concerns of negotiators should be whether the grant of differential treatment in that instance will increase sustainable development for the individual people of that country; if so, to what extent; and, if not, how an increase in development for the individual people of that country can be accomplished without differential treatment.

How would this alternative approach to special and differential treatment work in practice in the actual give and take of multilateral trade negotiations? Consider, for example, a request by a self-declared developing country for an exemption from a national treatment obligation that, without an exemption, would forbid it from discriminating in favour of its own domestic producers over foreign producers of a like product. In contrast to the past, future negotiations would centre on whether the grant of the request for an exemption would enable and advance the quest for sustainable development in the country making the request. This inquiry by the negotiators would therefore turn on whether sustainable development for the people of that country would be better secured over time by granting the request for an exemption or refusing it.

Some of the tools for carving the content of special and differential treatment on this new case-by-case basis are familiar. This approach applies different levels of expectation for developing countries' compliance with new obligations. It provides time frames allowing for gradual implementation of these obligations. But it is unique in that it replaces the goal of exemption from obligations with the goal of enablement to fulfill them, and puts data at the heart of these decisions. Doing so would fundamentally change the mentality of WTO Members when making determinations on SDT and would, for the first time, bring the functioning of the WTO on the central issue of development fully within the expressed intent of the Marrakesh Agreement, which highlights the necessity that development be sustainable.

For the first time, WTO negotiations would consider how to make SDT a *transitional* form of treatment truly aimed towards full compliance by developing countries with their WTO obligations. With this aim in mind, these negotiations would turn more and more towards how to make certain that developing countries have the resources they need to make the transition to full compliance. A harbinger of such negotiations is the added emphasis on technical assistance and capacity-building in the Trade Facilitation Agreement. The TFA is rightly seen by Canada, Norway, and others as a welcome glimpse of the future in facing the divide over the different stages of development among WTO Members.

Without question, technical assistance, capacity-building, and financial assistance can make an enormous difference for developing countries in achieving their development goals. Developed countries that continue to resist providing such help should be reminded that they have agreed that technological facilitation is one of the means of implementation for the Sustainable Development Goals.[25] The members of the United Nations – including all the Members of the WTO – have agreed in establishing the Sustainable Development Goals that, "Processes to facilitate the availability of appropriate knowledge globally, as well as capacity-building, are…critical" in meeting these targets.[26] Desperately needed even more by developing countries is financial assistance.[27] Thus, as a vital part of the resolution of the controversy over the development dimension in the WTO, there is an urgent need for an affirmative and binding obligation by developed countries to provide technical assistance, capacity-building, and financial assistance to developing countries to help them achieve sustainable freedom and development.

A new grand bargain

There will undoubtedly be challenges in reaching an agreement on a new approach to SDT. Foremost among these will be relinquishing the outdated dichotomy between developed and developing country Members of the WTO. The world has become far more complicated than that, as new players have emerged and thrived. The trade rules should reflect these changes. Changing the long-existing approach to the trade rules that is reflected in the traditional approach to SDT will be difficult. What is needed to begin is an acknowledgement that the previous approach has been insufficient in meeting the needs of the membership, and that special and differential treatment has contributed to this failure. To support reaching a new grand bargain on SDT, what is needed is an objective assessment of its operation, and a data-driven multilateral negotiation oriented towards sustainable development.

Although the WTO Secretariat has compiled a detailed report of the 183 provisions in the WTO agreements that give developing countries special rights, no official assessment has been made of whether or how SDT has helped developing countries. WTO Members should audit past provisions and evaluate their effectiveness. Such an exercise would be valuable on several fronts. First, it would motivate Members to take stock of where they stand, and to think through what they might need to fully meet their obligations, such as technical assistance. Second, it would help Members get a sense of how past grants of SDT enabled or inadvertently delayed their ability to take advantage of new commitments, allowing them to get a stronger grasp of the impact of these policy choices. Third, it would support an important goal of the WTO by improving transparency in this critical issue area. This would be of benefit not only to WTO Members but also to researchers who are trying to improve knowledge about this subject, and also to organisations that are seeking to help developing countries get the most out of the trading system. Only by sharing the experiences of developing countries can we better understand how best they can develop.

That said, there is no need to alter matters that have already been agreed. However, in crafting a new approach to SDT, there is space for creativity and boldness in future negotiations. The opportunity to move from discussing ideas about reform and actually implementing them is already before us. As of this writing, the WTO is engaged in multilateral talks on fisheries subsidies, which could prove to be the test case of the organisation's ability to adapt to this new trade landscape. For the most part, the WTO has not produced any new multilateral agreements since it was established. But, a multilateral solution is needed to discipline fisheries subsidies. In this particular case, a plurilateral agreement would do little to achieve the key objectives of the fisheries talks. Overfishing is by definition a global problem requiring a global solution. An estimated 37 percent of all the seafood produced in the world is traded internationally, which places this issue squarely within the scope of the WTO. Furthermore, the issue of fisheries best illustrates the modern challenges to trade, and the overlap of various issue areas. The fisheries negotiations are not just about subsidies. They are about environmental sustainability and development as well. How we navigate the intersection of these issues will be an important test of the WTO's ability to adapt to new circumstances.

Part of this changing landscape is the growth of emerging markets with significant shares of trade flows that challenges long-held assumptions about how to allocate special and differential treatment. In fact, 9 out of 15 of the largest marine capture fish producers are developing Members; China has been the top exporter of fish and fish products since 2002, and India has held the 4th spot since 2017. Despite this, China has been one of the most ardent defenders of SDT, regardless of particular development needs, including in fisheries. In a 2019 communication, China called for "reasonable policy space" in fisheries rules and "appropriate and effective special and differential treatment."[28]

Likewise, India has been reluctant to change the approach to SDT in the fisheries talks, and has called for more of the same – phase outs and blanket exemptions in some cases – this, even though India does not significantly subsidise its fisheries sector, but would like enough flexibility to do so in the future as that sector expands. Such thinking from developing countries is exactly why SDT has not always been about helping countries to develop but rather has been about creating and maintaining a mindset that certain WTO Members should be permanently exempted from meeting their WTO obligations. This, in turn, creates a *de facto* two-tiered trading system in which developing countries later complain that they have been denied access to developed country markets.

Furthermore, such religious adherence to SDT on the part of the larger developing Members of the WTO will undoubtedly have a negative impact on smaller Members that do not have the means to subsidise, but who heavily rely on fisheries for both subsistence and their livelihoods. Some proposals currently on the table for the fisheries talks favour an approach that requires Members that have a larger share of the global fisheries catch to take on greater reductions in their subsidies. But, even these proposals have been met with opposition from some developing country Members, particularly those with larger fishing fleets. As Alice Tipping has explained, "subsidization that encourages fishing that depletes stocks may ultimately undermine both poverty reduction and food security objectives and development interests. Ensuring that fish stocks are exploited sustainably is thus crucial if policy-makers want to ensure that development priorities can continue to be achieved in the medium and longer terms."[29]

The fisheries negotiations make clear beyond any other that dividing countries into two broad categories labelled "developed" and "developing," blurs important distinctions among developing countries. In addition, these negotiations are deeply tied to development, making it the ideal ground to experiment with a new way forward on SDT, which can also set the stage for a new grand bargain on differential treatment. It is worth reminding ourselves that these talks are directly linked to achieving one of the 17 United Nations Sustainable Development Goals, to "conserve and sustainably use the oceans, seas and marine resources for sustainable development."[30] Specific targets under this goal are to "prohibit certain forms of fisheries subsidies which contribute to overcapacity and overfishing, eliminate subsidies that contribute to illegal, unreported and unregulated fishing, and refrain from introducing new such subsidies," and to "end overfishing, illegal, unreported and unregulated fishing and destructive fishing practices and implement science-based management plans ...."[31]

The Hong Kong mandate identified poverty reduction, livelihood, and food security concerns, in addition to "the importance of this sector to development priories" as key factors to take into account for establishing SDT in fisheries negotiations.[32] This provides some guidance on how to evaluate the grant of SDT. In particular, if one of the goals of the talks is to reduce subsidies to large-scale industrial fishing vessels, while providing some flexibility to artisanal and small-scale fishing, a case can be made for how the latter aids in the reduction of poverty, supports a way of life, and ensures food security.

For example, the UN Food and Agriculture Organization and its partners developed the Nha Trang indicators to examine the contribution of small-scale aquaculture through a "sustainable livelihood" approach "to balance the use and/or development of the five types of livelihood capital or assets (natural, physical, human, financial and social)."[33] Through a number of case studies, researchers found "that small-scale aquaculture encourages formation of community farmer organizations, women's empowerment and voice in economic enterprise, networks and collective action," and also "fosters social harmony through the sharing of harvest and technical knowledge and expertise."[34] These are surely outcomes that support sustainable development, and a strong example of where SDT should be considered, and can be helpful. But again, it is only through an objective assessment of the data, and clearly tying the outcome of interest to development needs that we can start thinking of SDT through our alternative approach framework. The ample research done in the fisheries sector should provide ready reference to negotiators of what works for development and what does not. Ignoring the effort of experts in this field and turning the negotiations into simply another exercise of seeing how little each side can *give* for what it *gets* will set us back on making any meaningful progress in addressing the needs of developing countries at the WTO.

Lastly, any agreement on fisheries subsidies should incorporate an idea put forward by the European Union in its reform proposal, which suggests that SDT provisions could become a part of the WTO process of regular reviews of the trade policies of all WTO Members. This reform would bolster the monitoring function of the WTO, and it would offer additional support to the work of the committee that is established to monitor the agreement. If such assessments can be done through the trade policy review mechanism, it will also improve transparency in the implementation of new commitments, but also flag where developing Members may be falling short in meeting them. Where difficulty in implementation is a result of capacity constraints, the necessary tools and expertise should be provided to help those Members fulfill their obligations. It would be useful if this approach could be embedded in all future agreements, so that there is a regular review of SDT provisions that will shed more light on what works and what does not. At present, there has been little in the way of an empirical assessment of these provisions, and such an exercise could help establish better data for such analysis.

Many still assume there is a strong case for the current, exemption-focused approach to SDT, despite its "less-than-stellar record."[35] We contend that there is a strong case for SDT *only if it facilitates the transition towards development*. The right approach to SDT will embrace an objective assessment of human needs and will not try to insulate and isolate individuals and the enterprises for which they work in developing countries from the competition with foreign trade. The right approach will help empower the individual citizens of those countries to reap the full benefits of integration into the global trading system so they can flourish within the wider world. By contrast, further weakening the WTO-based multilateral trading system will not help developing countries but will harm them by postponing or even preventing their development.[36] The alternative approach that we outline above can provide a way forward on a new grand bargain to special and differential treatment that can live up to its promise for improving development outcomes. In addressing the development dimension, it must always be remembered: the goal is freedom.

Endnotes

1. Preamble, Marrakesh Agreement, para. 2.
2. Nairobi Ministerial Declaration, WT/MIN(15)DEC (December 19, 2015), para. 6–7.
3. Preamble, Marrakesh Agreement, para. 1.
4. "Transforming Our World: The 2030 Agenda for Sustainable Development," A/RES/70/1 (September 27, 2015).
5. "Our Common Future," Report of the World Commission on Environment and Development (1987), para. 27 (commonly known as the "Brundtland Report").
6. Amartya Sen, *The Idea of Justice* (Cambridge, MA: Harvard University Press, 2009), 249.
7. Ibid. at 251–252.
8. *See* James Bacchus, *Trade and Freedom* (London: Cameron May, 2004).

74 *Alternative approach to differential treatment*

9. William Easterly, *The Tyranny of Experts: Economists, Dictators, and the Forgotten Rights of the Poor* (New York: Basic Books, 2013), 7.
10. Patrick Low, Hamid Mamdouh, and Evan Rogerson, at 27.
11. Michael Hart and Bill Dymond, at 398.
12. Ibid. at 398, 404–405.
13. Ibid.
14. Patrick Low, Hamid Mamdouh, and Evan Rogerson, at 11.
15. Ibid.
16. Anabel González, "Bridging the Divide between Developed and Developing Countries in WTO Negotiations." (March 12, 2019), at https://www.piie.com/blogs/trade-investment-policy-watch/bridging-divide-between-developed-and-developing-countries-wto.
17. Amartya Sen, *Development as Freedom*, at 3.
18. Amartya Sen, *Development as Freedom*, at 3, 18.
19. On the Human Development Index, *see* United Nations Development Programme, at http://hdr.undp.org/en/content/human-development-index-hdi.
20. United Nations Development Programme, Human Development Reports, 2018 Statistical Update, at http://hdr.undp.org/en/2018-update.
21. Anabel González, "Revisiting 'special and differential treatment' in the WTO," East Asia Forum (March 26, 2019), at https://eastasiaforum.org/2019/03/26/revisiting-special-and-differential-treatment-in-WTO.
22. Joel Trachtman, "Can Special and Differential Treatment Reduce Poverty?" International Economic Law and Policy Blog (April 18, 2019), at https://worldtradelaw.typepad.com/ielpblog/2019/04/can-special-and-differential-treatment-reduce-poverty.
23. U.S. Statements Delivered by Ambassador Dennis Shea, WTO General Council Meeting (May 7, 2019), at https://geneva.usmission.gov/2019/05/08/ambassador-sheas-statement-at-the-wto-general-council-meeting-agenda-items-4-6-7/.
24. United Nations Conference on Trade and Development, "The Least Developed Countries Report 2019" (Geneva: UNCTAD, 2019), ii.
25. Transforming Our World: The 2030 Agenda for Sustainable Development, para. 70, A/RES/70/1 (September 27, 2015), para. 70.
26. Transforming Our World, para. 63.
27. Transforming Our World, paras. 62 and 63.
28. Communication from China, "A Cap-Based Approach to Address Certain Fisheries Subsidies that Contribute to Overcapacity and Overfishing," TN/RL/GEN/199 (June 4, 2019).
29. Alice Tipping, "Addressing the Development Dimension of an Overcapacity and Overfishing Subsidy Discipline in the WTO Fisheries Subsidies Negotiations," A Discussion Paper by IISD (January 2020), at https://www.iisd.org/system/files/publications/overfishing-discipline-wto-fisheries-subsidies.pdf.
30. United Nations Sustainable Development Goals, at https://sdgs.un.org/goals/goal14.
31. Ibid. at Targets 14.4 and 14.6.
32. World Trade Organization (WTO) *Ministerial Decision 2005WT/MIN(05)/DEC. 22 WTO* (December 22, 2005) https://www.wto.org/english/thewto_e/minist_e/min05_e/final_text_e.htm.

33. "The state of world fisheries and aquaculture" Rome: Food and Agriculture Organization (2018): 143, http://www.fao.org/documents/card/en/c/I9540EN/.
34. Ibid. at 144.
35. Hart and Dymond, "Special and Differential Treatment," 398, 404–405.
36. Ibid. at 398.

8 Conclusion

Assailed on all sides, the World Trade Organization (WTO) is in existential crisis. There are various aspects to this crisis. Yet, it cannot be resolved unless and until the role of the development dimension in trade is also resolved. Special and differential treatment (SDT) in the WTO has long been self-declared and undefined, and it remains so today. In no uncertain terms, the United States has voiced its desire for change in the ways the WTO affords SDT. Other countries, developed and developing alike, have added their voices to the debate both for and against reform. As this emerging debate has revealed, there is little agreement among WTO Members about when SDT is appropriate, what it should provide, or what its purpose should be in the multilateral trading system. And there is little evidence that SDT has furthered the aim of development that is central to the mission of the WTO.

Finding an alternative approach for determining the eligibility for, and the content of, SDT must be placed on the WTO negotiating agenda, and an early resolution to the dilemma of the development dimension should be found through new multilateral negotiations. That new approach should be developed now, perhaps by using the current negotiations on fisheries subsidies as a proving ground. Eventually, that new approach should become part of a "grand bargain" by the 164 members of the WTO that will renew the multilateral trading system, restore it as the centre of world trade, and reaffirm its purpose of fostering the full flourishing of human freedom through a sustainable global development that is spurred and enhanced by trade.

Index

Note: **Bold** page numbers refer to tables

Aggregate Measures of Support (AMS) 16
agreements 20, 24, 28, 29, 53, 60, 63, 64, 69, 72, 73
agricultural products 16, 29
agricultural trade 16
Article XXXVI 26
Article XXXVII 26
Article XXXVIII 26
Australia 63

Bagwell, Kyle 40
Bangladesh 50
barriers to trade 23, 24
Brazil 14, 50, 63, 67

Canada 19
case-by-case approach 61, 64–67
China 3, 12, 15, 16, 45, 46, 48, 50, 52, 53, 62, 63, 70; poverty in 3
communication 3, 6, 12, 17–19, 70
concessions 15, 23, 24, 38, 40, 60
Covid-19 pandemic 6, 46

Democratic Republic of Congo 50
developing countries 1–3, 15, 16, 25–29, 31, 34, 35, 40, 51, 53, 58, 60, 61, 65
development concept 14
dispute settlement 27, 31, 32, 52
Doha Declaration 30–31, 47
Doha Development Round 2, 9, 16, 30, 55

domestic economic growth 14
domestic policymaking 7
Dymond, Bill 35, 40, 58, 59

Easterly, William 57
economic transformations 46
Enabling Clause 27
Ethiopia 50
European Union 20, 72

fisheries negotiations 71
France 50
freer trade 35, 37, 42

Gao, Henry 51, 52
Garcia, Frank 23
General Agreement on Tariffs and Trade (GATT) 23–27, 29
Generalized System of Preferences (GSP) 27, 28
Germany 63
global economy, China's emergence 45–54
González, Anabel 3, 60, 63
gross domestic product (GDP) 48, **49**
gross national income (GNI) 8, 48, **49**, 50

Hart, Michael 35, 40, 58, 59
Hoekman, Bernard 47
human development 14
Human Development Index (HDI) 8, 62–63
human freedom 14, 76

India 14, 50, 62, 63, 71
Indonesia 14, 62
Irwin, Douglas 36

Japan 63

Lamp, Nicolas 34
least developed countries (LDCs) 7, 8, 25–26, 30, 39, 65–67
Low, Patrick 34, 58–59

Mamdouh, Hamid 34, 58, 59
Man-Keung Tang 41
Marrakesh Agreement 56–58, 63, 68
Mexico 63
multilateral trade negotiations 4, 24; Doha Development Round 30
multilateral trading system 2, 3, 7, 8, 16, 17, 25, 34, 52, 53, 55, 57–58, 60, 76

Nigeria 50
non-reciprocity concept 25–27, 35
Norway 63

obligations 1, 2, 15, 16, 31, 32, 40, 41, 58, 61, 65, 68, 71
The Open Society and Its Enemies 42
Organisation for Economic Co-operation and Development (OECD) 8, 48
Ornelas, Emanuel 38, 39
overfishing 70

Pakistan 14
Panagariya, Arvind 36, 37
Pauwelyn, Joost 39
policy space 15
Popper, Sir Karl 42
poverty 6, 57, 62; reduction 72
Prebisch, Raul 42
protectionism 35, 37–40

reasonable policy space 70
reciprocity concept 15, 24, 25, 27, 34, 38
Ricardo, David 38
Rogerson, Evan 34, 58, 59

self-declaration 2, 6, 7, 15, 64, 65, 67, 68
Sen, Amartya 14–15, 48, 56, 61, 62
Shang-Jin Wei 41
Shea, Dennis 65
Singer, Hans 42
Smith, Adam 38
South Africa 62
South Korea 50
special and differential treatment 6, 7, 17, 20, 28, 31, 34, 37, 39, 47, 52, 55, 57–61, 65, 67, 68; alternative approach to 55–75; evolution of 23–33; failure of current approach 34–44; new grand bargain 69–73; provisions 8, 30, 31
Staiger, Robert 40
sustainable development 57, 62
Sustainable Development Goals (SDGs) 17, 56, 57, 66, 69
Switzerland 63

Tipping, Alice 71
Trachtman, Joel 63, 64
trade: barriers 23, 24, 35, 39; confrontation 52; grievances 52; liberalisation 24, 39, 47; liberalising 16; negotiations 23, 24, 26, 61, 64; obligations 28, 29; regime 58; rules 26, 47, 69; sectors 63, 66, 67; trading system 2, 25–27, 35, 59, 60, 70
Trade Facilitation Agreement (TFA) 52, 68
trade-off 35
Trump, Donald 2, 3, 17, 40, 45, 60, 65

UK 50
unilateral trade liberalisation 24
United Nations Conference on Trade and Development (UNCTAD) 46
United Nations Development Programme (UNDP) 8, 15, 39
United Nations Sustainable Development Goals 17, 56, 71
United States 1–3, 6–9, 12–15, 17, 24, 27, 36, 40, 45–46, 51–53, 60, 62, 63, 65, 76

United States proposal 45, 47, 52, 62; developed countries, balance and pragmatism 18–20; developing countries 12–17; responses 12–22; and special and differential treatment 6–11
Uruguay Round trade agreements 2, 26, 28–29, 51

Vietnam 63

World Bank 6, 8, 62
world economy 3, 6, 7, 57; integration of 3
World Trade Organization (WTO) 1–4, 6, 7, 12–15, 28–31, 41, 51–53, 55, 57–61, 64, 65, 68–72, 76; Agreement on Technical Barriers to Trade 19; agreements 19, 47, 52, 55–57, 67–69; dispute settlement 31, 32; General Agreement on Trade in Services 19; least developed countries (LDCs) 26, 30; ministerial conference 29; obligations 40, 41; rules-based trading system 3; Trade Facilitation Agreement (TFA) 19; trading system 66
world trading system 2, 12

Zhao, Weihuan 51